Politics in America

Politics in America

A Guide to the Two-Party System

Frank P. Daversa

authorHOUSE®

AuthorHouse™
1663 Liberty Drive
Bloomington, IN 47403
www.authorhouse.com
Phone: 1-800-839-8640

Politics in America: A Guide to the Two-Party System

First Edition

Cover design by Frank P. Daversa
Cover illustration copyright © 2012 by Frank P. Daversa
Cover image courtesy of www.ClipartOf.com

Published by AuthorHouse   10/08/2012

ISBN: 978-1-4772-7677-8 (sc)

Library of Congress Control Number: 2012918374

An informed electorate is our nation's best resource.

Contents

Introduction 1

Chapter 1: Constituency 3

Chapter 2: Party History 7

Chapter 3: Party Ideology 30

Chapter 4: Sample Legislation 44

Chapter 5: Editorials 77

Chapter 6: Conclusion 124

INTRODUCTION

Citizens of the United States enjoy certain basic rights: the right to free speech, the right to own land, the right to trial by jury, and the right to peaceably assemble, just to name a few. But there is no more fundamental privilege than the right to vote. The right to choose our elected officials forms the very basis of our democratic system of government. This is true at the national as well as the state and local levels. We should be grateful for this right—many countries still deny their people the right to free and fair elections. Indeed, it is our responsibility as citizens to exercise this privilege come election time. Provided you are 18 years of age or over, register to vote if you have not done so already.

Politics is an inescapable fact of life in America. It impacts many governmental policies, which in turn impact our everyday lives. Tax policies affect the amount of income we owe the government. Federal and state economic policies affect the job market. Defense policies affect whether and how we wage wars abroad. Food and Drug Administration (FDA) policies affect the safety of the foods we eat and the drugs we take. The national party voted into power after each election is responsible for regulating these policies. They are the reason why voting is so important.

This book is intended primarily for readers with a small to moderate familiarity with politics. Politics influence your vote one way or another, and it is the intention of this book to illustrate how. It provides backgrounds of the Democratic and Republican Parties, their basic philosophies, examples of congressional acts passed into law, and a discussion of relevant issues in the political arena today. It draws upon excerpts compiled from online newspapers and sources as well as noted cable news programs to provide insightful commentary. As a voter, education is your greatest asset.

CHAPTER 1
CONSTITUENCY

Merriam-Webster defines politics as "the art or science of government."[1] Government, in turn, is defined as "the complex of political institutions, laws, and customs through which the function of governing is carried out."[2] To the average person, politics in America can seem fairly complicated. There are three branches of government at both the federal and state levels and a myriad of laws that have to be followed. A nominee is chosen from a field of candidates during a primary, and then a candidate is chosen from each level of government during the general election. While there can be multiple parties to choose from in congressional elections, the field is typically limited to two in presidential elections. This is because our electoral process constitutes a winner-takes-all system. (While other parties are present in any given presidential election, their election results are generally nominal.)

A two-party system certainly simplifies the process, which is one of the main reasons why it is so successful in America. For many voters, allegiance to a party is determined by family. Those who grew up in a predominantly conservative household will tend to vote Republican, while those who grew up in a predominantly progressive household will tend to vote Democratic.

---

[1] See http://www.merriam-webster.com/dictionary/politics.

[2] See http://www.merriam-webster.com/dictionary/government?show=0&t=1333928696.

There are also the core principles of each party to consider. The Democratic Party is the oldest party in existence. Today it comprises:

- <u>Liberal Democrats</u>, who advocate strong civil liberties, fair trade, more moderate economic policies, and a less militaristic foreign policy.
- <u>Progressive Democrats</u>, who advocate relatively centrist economic and left-wing social agendas, universal health care, and revitalization of the national infrastructure.
- <u>Centrists</u>, who advocate the use of military force, a reduction in government welfare, and tax cuts.
- <u>The Christian left</u>, which advocates social justice, welfare, universal health care, education, and foreign aid.
- <u>Conservative Democrats</u>, who advocate centrist positions on social/cultural and neo-liberal fiscal issues. They are similar to their liberal Republican counterparts in that both became political minorities after their respective political parties underwent a major political realignment following civil rights legislation in 1964.
- <u>Libertarian Democrats</u>, who advocate civil rights, separation of church and state, and reduction of the national debt. As opposed to traditional Libertarians, they are more closely aligned with Democratic Party positions, including the Democrats' economic agenda. They oppose gun control, the War on Drugs, protectionism, corporate welfare, governmental borrowing, and an interventionist foreign policy.
- <u>Unions</u>, which advocate passage of the Employee Free Choice Act, an act that would make it easier for

employees to join a union and increase penalties for employer violations of the National Labor Relations Act. Other important issues for labor unions include support for industrial policies (including fair trade) that sustain unionized manufacturing jobs, raise the minimum wage, and promote broad social programs such as social security and universal health care.

- Ethnic minorities, who advocate affirmative action, civil rights, economic growth, and immigration reform.[3]

The Republican Party was formed in 1854 and today comprises:

- Fiscal conservatives, who advocate low taxes, a balanced budget, deregulation, and restricted government spending and national debt.
- Social conservatives, who believe in preserving traditional Christian values.
- Neoconservatives, who advocate promoting democracy around the world by military action, if necessary.
- Moderates, who advocate reasonable limits to issues and are temperate in their approach to topics. They are characterized by political or social beliefs that are neither extreme nor partisan, such as same-sex marriage and gay adoption, gun control laws, more environmental regulation and anti-climate-change measures, more federal spending on public education, fewer restrictions on legal immigration,

---

[3]　See http://en.wikipedia.org/wiki/
Factions_in_the_Democratic_Party_(United_States).

civil rights laws, embryonic stem cell research, and anti-war policies.[4]

- <u>Libertarians</u>, who advocate individual liberty as the basic moral principle of society. They promote strict limits to government activity, maximizing political freedom, and free-market capitalism as their main tenets.[5]

The question arises: Who should you vote for? Much of the answer depends on your beliefs. Those who believe in civil rights, a strong central government, gun control, strong government regulation, and social programs that benefit the needy and elderly tend to vote Democratic. Those who believe in low taxes, limited government intervention, unfettered free-market capitalism, limited gun control, and fewer government regulations tend to vote Republican. Voting is a personal decision with many factors involved. The purpose of this book is to make you aware of those factors.

---

[4] See http://en.wikipedia.org/wiki/
Factions_in_the_Republican_Party_(United_States).

[5] See http://en.wikipedia.org/wiki/Republican_party_(United_States).

Chapter 2
Party History

A historical overview of each party is valuable in achieving a better understanding of how the Democratic and Republican Parties operate. They started out quite different than they are today. Note: This chapter is quoted directly from the World Book Encyclopedia unless otherwise indicated.

DEMOCRATIC PARTY

The origin of the Democratic Party is not certain. Some historians trace its start to a party called the Democratic-Republican Party that Thomas Jefferson created during the 1790s . . . Most historians, however, regard Andrew Jackson's presidential campaign organization, formed in 1828, as the beginning of the Democratic Party as it is known today.

[The Democratic-Republican Party ascended to power in the election of 1800.] Jefferson served as president from 1801 to 1809, and other Democratic-Republicans held the presidency from 1809 to 1825. After 1816, however, the Democratic-Republican Party split into several groups and fell apart as a national organization. Jackson became the favorite of one of these groups and gained great popularity. After losing a bid for the presidency in 1824, he easily won election in 1828 and swept to reelection in 1832. By about 1830, Jackson and his followers were called Democrats. By the late 1830s, top Jacksonian Democrats had turned

Jackson's loose organization into an effective national party—the Democratic Party.

Jacksonian policies appealed to a wide variety of voters ... They had in common a strong belief in states' rights and a firm faith in limited government . . . But Democrats also disagreed over banking policies, slavery, tariff rates, and other issues. Under Jackson and Vice President Martin Van Buren, who became president in 1837, the Democrats expanded the *spoils system*—the use of government jobs and contracts to reward campaign workers and party officials. The Democrats won the presidential election of 1844 with James K. Polk. In 1852, they won with Franklin Pierce, and in 1856, with James Buchanan. They also controlled Congress during most of the 1840s and 1850s.

The slavery issue, more than any other, divided the Democrats. During Polk's administration, from 1845 to 1849, vast new territories in the West became part of the United States . . . Southerners wanted to extend slavery into the new lands, but many Northerners urged Congress to prohibit it. Fierce debates led to division within the party and to sectional hostility between North and South. Congressional leaders, such as Democratic Senator Stephen A. Douglas of Illinois, worked for legislation that would satisfy both sides. They won passage of the Compromise of 1850, which, for a time, quieted both party and sectional differences.

Hostility flared again after Congress passed the Kansas-Nebraska Act of 1854. In this act, Douglas had provided for "popular sovereignty," which let settlers decide for themselves whether a new state would permit slavery. The act pleased few people. It led to renewed hostility between North and South and caused the Democratic Party to split apart.

In 1860, Northern Democrats nominate Douglas for president. Southern Democrats chose John C. Breckinridge. Both Democratic candidates lost to Abraham Lincoln, the candidate of the new Republican Party. In 1860 and 1861, 11 Southern states seceded from the Union. In April 1861, shortly after the seventeenth state had withdrawn, the American Civil War began. During the Civil War, the Northern Democrats divided. Some, known as the War Democrats, supported Lincoln and the war. The Peace Democrats, especially those known as "Copperheads," opposed Lincoln and the war. In the election of 1864, many War Democrats joined the Republican Party to form the Union Party. Andrew Johnson, a War Democrat, became Lincoln's vice presidential running mate. The Peace Democrats nominated General George B. McClellan for the presidency. Lincoln won the election. After Lincoln' assassination in 1865, Vice President Johnson became president.

After the Civil War, the popularity of the Democratic Party declined. Republicans condemned the Democrats, claiming they were disloyal to the Union during the war. Under Johnson's leadership, the Democrats attacked the Radical Republicans' [(i.e., abolitionists')] plan for Reconstruction, the process by which the Union restored relations with the Confederate states after their defeat . . . Among other actions, the Republicans (1) denied the vote to Southerners who had fought against the Union, and (2) gave the vote to Southern blacks. Enraged white Southerners later regained power and deprived blacks of the vote. These white Southerners believed that the Republicans opposed most Southern beliefs. Thus, the Democratic "Solid South" was born . . .

As Civil War issues faded, there seemed to be less and less difference between the Democratic and Republican parties. But the Democrats were distinguished by their support of lower tariffs. The Democrats' image as supporters of states' rights and limited government appealed to white Southerners, small farmers, and many Northerners. Drawing on this appeal in 1884, Grover Cleveland became the first Democrat elected president since 1856. He narrowly lost the presidency to Benjamin Harrison in 1888, but he regained it in another close race in 1892.

Tremendous changes had reshaped the economy since the Civil War. Railroads had expanded to carry goods to farmers and farm products to city workers. Vast business and industrial empires had appeared. Politicians knew little about business growth, depressions, or economic theories. Democrats and Republicans favored a policy of *laissez-faire* (non-regulation), and the government left business in the hands of business owners. Neither party seemed aware of hardships that industrialization brought to many people.

In 1893, shortly after Cleveland began his second term as president, a major economic depression struck the nation . . . Confused by the problems of an increasingly industrialized society, Cleveland followed a laissez-faire policy even as farmers faced ruin, city workers went on strike and unemployment rose. The amount of money in circulation became the major campaign issue in the election of 1896. Most Democrats supported *free silver*, a plan to put more money in circulation by coining silver dollars to help the nation's economic problems . . . Most Republicans favored the *gold standard*, a system in which the nation would define its currency as worth a certain quantity of gold. William Jennings Bryan, a supporter of free silver, won the Democratic presidential nomination with his famous "cross of gold" speech. He campaigned energetically and won wide support in the South and West—but ran poorly in the East and lost the election. Bryan lost again in 1900. Another Democrat, Alton B. Parker, was defeated in 1904, and Bryan lost again in 1908.

. . . In 1912, a split in the Republican Party enabled the Democratic candidate, Woodrow Wilson, to win the presidency . . . In addition, for the first time in 20 years, the Democrats gained control of both houses of Congress. In 1916, Wilson won reelection, and the Democrats retained control of Congress. Wilson introduced a number of reforms during his time in office. He wanted to eliminate monopoly and special privilege from American business, but without expanding the regulatory power of the federal government. He worked to restore fair competition and called for Americans to have a "new freedom" to prosper. During his first administration, he signed into law such reform legislation as the Clayton Antitrust Act, the Federal Trade Commission Act, and the Underwood Tariff Act.

During Wilson's second administration, World War I (1914-1918) overshadowed his drive for further reform. Wilson directed the nation's energy to the defeat of Germany. After the war, he called for the United States to join the League of Nations. Wilson, the chief planner of the League, believed that the international organization would help prevent future wars. Most Democrats supported the League, but some joined with conservative Republicans and blocked U.S. membership.

During the 1920s, the Democrats failed to win the presidency or to gain control of either house in Congress. The United States seemed prosperous, as business boomed and industry expanded. But beneath the surface of prosperity lay much economic disorder. Neither business nor government took action in spite of the danger signals occurring in 1927 and 1928.

In 1928, questions of religion and the prohibition of alcohol divided the Northern and Southern wings of the Democratic Party. Many Southern Democrats were Protestants who supported Prohibition, and they were wary of the party's presidential nominee, New York Governor Alfred E. Smith. Smith, a Roman Catholic, wanted to repeal the 18th Amendment to the Constitution, which prohibited the sale of alcoholic beverages. Lack of unity among the Democrats helped Herbert Hoover, the Republican nominee, win a landslide victory.

In 1929, the United States suffered the worst stock market crash in its history. As economic conditions worsened, Hoover's Republican administration provided aid for some failing banks, railroads, and agricultural organizations. However, Hoover was committed to the concept of "rugged individualism," and he refused to offer direct government aid to people in need of relief from the economic disaster.

. . . The Great Depression brought a revolution in the fortunes of the Democratic Party. Democrats won every presidential election of the 1930s and 1940s and controlled Congress for most of that period. Franklin D. Roosevelt won the elections of 1932, 1936, 1940, and 1944, becoming the only person to win the presidency four times.

Roosevelt was the dominant figure of the Depression years. He did even more than Wilson to convert the Democrats from a party of states' rights and limited government to one of national reform. During the 1932 campaign, he had promised Americans a "new deal" that included economic relief, recovery, and reform, and a better life for what he called the "forgotten man." Roosevelt followed through on the promises on his New Deal program by greatly expanding the role of government. Under the New Deal, the federal government imposed numerous business regulations and passed laws to help the needy. Roosevelt's personality and confidence made him a hero to millions.

Most farmers, intellectuals, unemployed workers, wage earners, and members of minority groups supported the New Deal and voted Democratic. Most Southerners and residents of big cities also backed the party. But conservatives—both Democrats and Republicans—believed that the federal government was taking far too great a role in people's lives. In response to Roosevelt's 1937 plan to reorganize the Supreme Court of the United States, many Southern Democrats joined with Republicans in a conservative coalition . . . The coalition blocked many Democratic attempts at reform.

During World War II (1939-1945), Roosevelt turned the nation's efforts toward defeating Germany and Japan. Roosevelt died in 1945. Vice President Harry S. Truman succeeded him as president. Truman continued the policies of the New Deal, calling his program the Fair Deal. He fought for civil rights for African Americans and for a national medical insurance plan. However, Southern Democrats often joined Republicans to block Truman's efforts. In 1948, some Southern Democrats formed the

States' Rights Democratic Party, or Dixiecrat Party, to oppose Truman . . . But he won a surprising victory over the Republican candidate, Thomas E. Dewey.

In both 1952 and 1956, the Democratic presidential candidate, Adlai E. Stevenson, lost to Dwight D, Eisenhower, one of the nation's greatest heroes of World War II. Yet the Democrats controlled Congress for the last six of Eisenhower's eight years in office.

. . . Senator John F. Kennedy of Massachusetts won the presidency in 1960, defeating the Republican nominee, Vice President Richard M. Nixon. Kennedy called for numerous reforms in his program, which he named the New Frontier. Democrats outnumbered Republicans in both houses of Congress, but conservative Southern Democrats frequently joined Republicans to defeat bills that Kennedy supported.

. . . Vice President Lyndon B. Johnson became president after Kennedy was assassinated in 1963. In 1964, Johnson won a full term as president with a landslide victory over his Republican opponent, Barry M. Goldwater. Johnson worked hard for the program that Kennedy had begun. Johnson called on the nation to join him in building what he termed the Great Society. Congress approved Johnson's requests for aid to cities and education, landmark civil rights legislation, greater Social Security benefits, and tax cuts.

. . . By 1966, the Vietnam War, and the nationwide disagreement over it, overshadowed Johnson's Great Society program. The war divided many Americans into "hawks," who supported U.S. involvement in Vietnam, and "doves," who opposed it. Johnson announced that he would not run for reelection in 1968, and Vice President Hubert H. Humphrey became the Democratic nominee . . . The Republican candidate, Richard M. Nixon, won the presidency, but the Democrats kept control of Congress. Much of Nixon's success in the election was credited to his "Southern strategy," in which he appealed to conservative white Southerners. Nixon's emphasis on patriotism, law and order, and a slower approach to school integration helped erode the support that Democrats long had enjoyed in the South . . .

In the 1972 election, the Democrats nominated [George S.] McGovern, and the Republicans renominated Nixon. Nixon won a landslide victory. However, in 1974, Nixon resigned from the presidency rather than face impeachment for the Watergate scandal . . . Vice President Gerald R. Ford succeeded him.

. . . Jimmy Carter, the Democratic nominee, defeated Ford in the 1976 presidential election. The Democrats also retained control of Congress. In the 1980 election, however, Carter lost his bid for a second term. He was defeated by former California Governor Ronald Reagan, the Republican candidate. The Democrats also lost the Senate to the Republicans, though they kept control of the House.

Walter F. Mondale, Carter's vice president, became the Democratic presidential nominee in 1984. His running mate, Representative Geraldine A. Ferraro of New York, was the first woman vice presidential candidate of a major U.S. political party. However, Reagan easily won a second term, and the Republicans retained control of the Senate.

The election of 1986 gave Democrats control of both houses of Congress. In 1988, Massachusetts Governor Michael S. Dukakis won the Democratic presidential nomination. He lost the election to Republican Vice President George H. W. Bush, but the Democrats retained control of Congress.

In 1992, Governor Bill Clinton of Arkansas, the Democratic candidate, defeated Bush and independent candidate Ross Perot in the presidential election. But in 1994, the Democrats lost both houses of Congress to the Republicans. The shift in control marked the first time since January 1955 that the Republicans controlled both houses. In 1996, Clinton was reelected, defeating Republican Robert J. Dole. However, the Republicans kept control of Congress in 1996 and 1998.

. . . Vice President Al Gore was the Democratic candidate in 2000. His running mate, Connecticut Senator Joseph I. Lieberman, was the first Jewish vice presidential candidate of a major U.S. party. Gore lost to his Republican opponent, Texas Governor George W. Bush, in one of the closest presidential races in U.S. history.

In 2004, Bush won reelection, defeating Senator John F. Kerry of Massachusetts, the Democratic nominee. During his second term, Bush's public approval ratings fell, partly as a result of opposition to the Iraq War, which had begun in 2003. The Republican Party also experienced internal divisions over such issues as immigration, deficit spending, and lobbying reform.

In the 2006 Congressional elections, the Democrats won control of both houses of Congress for the first time since 1994. The victory enabled California Representative Nancy Pelosi to become the first female speaker of the House . . . . Political experts attributed the Democratic gains in part to public dissatisfaction with the Bush administration's handling of the Iraq War, as well as to scandals involving Republican lawmakers. A number of moderate candidates helped the Democratic Party compete in more conservative districts.

In the 2008 presidential election, [Senator Barack] Obama defeated his Republican opponent, Arizona Senator John McCain. Obama became the nation's first African American president. [The Great Recession] struck in the months before the election [and] contributed to the Democratic victory.[6]

In the 2010 elections, the Democratic Party lost control of the House, but kept a small majority in the Senate. It also lost its majority in state legislatures and state governorships. Some of the party's key 21st century national platform issues include combatting terrorism, homeland security, health care access expansion, labor rights, environmentalism, and the preservation of liberal government programs.

In 2010, Gallup polling found that 31% of Americans identified themselves as Democrats, 29% as Republicans, and 38% as independents.[7]

"Democratic Party" from the *World Book Encyclopedia* © 2012 World Book, Inc. By permission of the publisher. www.worldbook.com. All rights reserved. This article may not be reproduced in whole or in part in any form without prior written permission from World Book, Inc.

REPUBLICAN PARTY

[The] origin of the Republican Party dates back to the strong opposition to the Kansas-Nebraska Bill of 1854. The bill permitted slavery in the new territories of Kansas and Nebraska if people there voted for it.

---

[6]   The World Book Encyclopedia, (Chicago, IL: World Book, Inc., 2012), Volume 5, pp. 124-128.

[7]   See http://en.wikipedia.org/wiki/Democratic_Party_(United_States).

The Republican Party grew out of a series of anti-slavery meetings held throughout the North to protest the Kansas-Nebraska Bill. One such meeting was held by Alvan E. Bovay, a leading Whig, on February 28, 1854, in Ripon, Wisconsin. This meeting passed a resolution declaring that a new party—the Republican Party—would be organized if Congress passed the Kansas-Nebraska Bill.

Bovay held a second meeting in Ripon on March 20, after the Senate had approved the bill. The 53 men at this meeting appointed a committee to form the new party. Congress passed the Kansas-Nebraska Act on May 30. On July 6, at a party meeting in Jackson, Michigan, the delegates formally adopted the name *Republican*.

The new party had chiefly sectional appeal. Few Southern voters supported the Republicans, because almost all Southerners wanted to expand slavery, not restrict it. Many Northerners supported the party. But some feared that the extreme antislavery views of such Republican leaders as Senator Charles Sumner of Massachusetts threatened the Union.

[In] the election of 1856, the Republicans chose John Charles Freemont, a dashing young explorer and soldier, as their first presidential candidate. During the campaign, antislavery and proslavery groups fought in Kansas. The chief campaign issue became "bleeding Kansas." Democrats predicted that the South would secede from the Union if the antislavery Freemont won.

The voting reflected the sectional appeal of the Democratic and Republican Parties. Freemont won 11 northern states. His Democratic opponent, James Buchanan, carried 19 states—including every Southern state except Maryland—and won.

. . . After the Republican defeat in 1856, party leaders realized that they could not win the presidency on just the slavery issue. To broaden their appeal, Republican endorsed construction of a transcontinental railroad system and federal aid to improve harbors and rivers. They also promised to open western land for settlement, to raise U.S. tariff rates, and to permit slavery where it already existed.

In 1860, Republicans chose Abraham Lincoln, a lanky, self-educated Illinois lawyer, as their presidential candidate. Lincoln had received national attention by expressing moderate antislavery views in his debates with Illinois Senator Stephen A. Douglas, a Democrat. Lincoln easily won the election, even though he received less than 40 percent of the popular vote. The Democrats had split over the slavery issue. Northern Democrats nominated Douglas, and Southern Democrats chose Vice President John C. Breckinridge.

The American Civil War began in April 1861. Most Southerners believed the election of Lincoln justified secession. In 1860 and 1861—both before and after the shooting started—11 Southern states left the Union and formed the Confederate States of America. Above all, Lincoln wanted to save the Union. But many Republicans—the so-called Radical Republicans—made the abolition of slavery their main goal. Many Northern Democrats supported Lincoln and the war and were called War Democrats.

Lincoln tried to bring all groups of both parties together, but he succeeded only partly. By 1864, Lincoln's chances of reelection looked doubtful. To stress the national character of the war—and to gain more supporters—the Republican Party used the name *Union Party* in the 1864 election. It nominated Andrew Johnson, a War Democrat, for vice president. With the help of Northern military victories just before the election, Lincoln won a second term.

On April 9, 1865, Confederate General Robert E. Lee surrendered to Union General Ulysses S. Grant. Five days later, Lincoln was assassinated.

Johnson hoped to follow Lincoln's moderate plan of Reconstruction. But the Radical Republicans in Congress favored harsh punishment for the South. The Radicals dominated Congress after the congressional elections of 1866. They divided the South into five military districts, deprived former Confederate soldiers of the vote, and gave the vote to former slaves.

The dispute over Reconstruction hardened political loyalties along sectional lines. Most Northern Republicans supported the Radical Republicans who, by 1868, felt strong enough to drop the Union Party label. Many Northern Democrats also backed Republican policies. Southerners, however, rejected Republican leadership. As a result, Reconstruction led to the birth of the Democratic "Solid South." The Democrats dominated elections at all levels in the region . . .

The Republicans nominated Grant, the great Union war hero, for president in 1868, and he won an easy victory. Grant won reelection in 1872, but by this time many voters had become alarmed over corruption in both business and government. A depression in 1873 helped the Democrats win a sweeping victory in the congressional elections of the next year.

In 1876, the Republicans nominated a cautious reformer, Rutherford B. Hayes. A group of conservative

Republicans called *Stalwarts* opposed Hayes because he favored civil service reform and friendly relations with the South. Hayes and his followers became known as *Half-Breeds*. Samuel J. Tilden, the Democratic candidate, won more popular votes than Hayes, but the election was disputed. A special commission declared Hayes the winner by one vote. The Democrats accepted the verdict only because the Republicans had promised to end Reconstruction and withdraw federal troops from the South. Hayes kept the promise.

Political inactivity marked the 1880s and 1890s. Both major parties failed to face the problems resulting from the rapid industrialization that followed the Civil War. Many industrial monopolies set high prices for their products and services. Economic power became centered with a few wealthy business leaders, and farmers and wage earners suffered increasingly hard times.

In 1880, Republican James A. Garfield won the presidency. He was assassinated in 1881, only a few months after taking office, and Vice President Chester A. Arthur, a Stalwart, succeeded him. Arthur surprised his fellow Stalwarts by supporting civil service reform. In 1883, Congress passed the Pendleton Act, which established the merit system in the civil service.

In 1884, the Republican presidential candidate, James G. Blaine, narrowly lost to Grover Cleveland. The party made the protective tariff its chief campaign issue in 1888 and won the presidency with Benjamin Harrison. In 1890, the McKinley Tariff pushed tariffs higher than they had ever been before. Dissatisfaction with the tariff helped Cleveland defeat Harrison in 1892.

The money issue dominated the election of 1896. A third party, the Populist Party, had appeared during the early 1890s. The populists demanded that government increase the amount of money in circulation by permitting unlimited coinage of silver . . . Many Democrats joined the Populists in their demand for silver coinage. In 1896, the Democrats nominated William Jennings Bryan, the leading silver spokesman, for president. The Republican candidate, William McKinley, supported a currency backed by gold. McKinley won the election.

Economic conditions improved rapidly during the late 1890s. The U.S. victory in the Spanish-American War also gained support for the Republicans. McKinley defeated Bryan again in 1900. Six months into his second term, however, McKinley was assassinated. Vice President Theodore Roosevelt succeeded him.

. . ."Teddy" Roosevelt supported much reform legislation. He brought suits against several large monopolies and crusaded for honesty in government. Roosevelt also sponsored a conservation policy, laws to protect the American public from impure food and drugs, and legislation to regulate railroad rates.

In 1908, Roosevelt chose Secretary of War William Howard Taft to succeed him and continue his policies. Taft easily beat Bryan, who ran for the third time as the Democratic nominee. Taft brought many more suits against monopolies than Roosevelt had. But Taft, by nature quieter and more conservative than Roosevelt, lost favor with Republican progressives. He faced open hostility from the progressives after signing into law the high Payne-Aldrich Tariff in 1909. By 1912, Taft no longer led a united party, and the progressives turned to Roosevelt, who wanted to be president again. After the Republicans renominated Taft, Roosevelt left the party and formed the Progressive, or "Bull Moose," Party. The Republican split helped Woodrow Wilson, the Democratic candidate, win the election.

The Republicans began to reunite after their defeat, and in 1916, most of them supported the party candidate, Charles Evans Hughes. But some backed Wilson because he had promised progressive legislation and had kept the nation out of World War I, which had begun in 1914. Wilson won reelection by a close margin. A month after he took office for the second time, the United States went to war against Germany. By the congressional elections of 1918, the Republicans had reunited, and they gained control of Congress. After the war, the Republican-controlled Senate rejected American membership in the League of Nations . . .

During the Roaring Twenties, the Republicans won every presidential and congressional election. In 1920, the party's candidate, Warren G. Harding, promised a return to "normalcy." Americans, weary of wartime controls and world problems, wanted just that—and Harding won in a landslide. The nation's economy boomed during the 1920s as business and industry expanded. Successive Republican administrations helped big business by keeping government spending and taxes low and by raising tariffs.

After Harding's death in 1923, congressional investigations revealed corruption in several government departments during his administration. But the exposures did not prevent Harding's successor, Vice President Calvin Coolidge, from easily winning the 1924 election. Coolidge's administration seemed to reflect the largely anti-foreign, anti-immigration, anti-labor mood of the nation.

In 1928, the Republicans turned to Herbert Hoover, Coolidge's Secretary of Commerce. Hoover easily defeated his Democratic opponent, Alfred E. Smith, but Smith carried most of the largest cities. Soon after Hoover took office in 1929, the worst stock market crash in the nation's history occurred. The Great Depression followed. Hoover tried to stop the Depression but could not, and he lost badly in 1932 to the Democratic candidate, Franklin D. Roosevelt. Hoover's defeat reduced the Republicans to a hard core of business leaders, Midwestern farmers, and conservative workers.

After the Great Depression, the Republican Party remained the minority party for a generation. Roosevelt led the nation through the economic crisis with a massive federal program called the New Deal . . . The Republicans, far outnumbered in both houses of Congress, took little action against his policies. The 1936 Republican Party platform criticized the New Deal, but Roosevelt won by a landslide over Alfred M. Landon. By the election of 1940, World War II (1939-1945) had started. The Republicans nominated Wendell L. Willkie and continued to attack the New Deal, but Roosevelt easily won a third term. The United States entered the war in 1941. Roosevelt defeated Thomas E. Dewey in 1944 and became the only candidate to be elected president four times.

In the 1930s and 1940s, many Republicans accepted the idea of federal welfare programs and of U.S. leadership in world affairs. They also accepted U.S. membership in the United Nations, formed in 1945. Vice President Harry S. Truman became president after the death of Roosevelt in 1945. The Republicans expected to win the 1948 election easily, and they nominated Dewey again. But Truman won a surprise victory.

. . . Dwight D. Eisenhower, a U.S. Army general and World War II hero, sought the Republican nomination for the 1952 election. He ran partly to prevent Ohio Senator Robert A. Taft, a conservative isolationist, from becoming the nominee. Eisenhower gained the nomination and easily won the general election, defeating Adlai E. Stevenson. Eisenhower carried four Southern states and broke the Democratic Solid South for the first time in over 20 years. Voters turned to Eisenhower for a variety of reasons. Many voted Republican because of dissatisfaction with the government's conduct of the Korean War (1950-1953). Others believed charges that the Democrats had harbored Communists in high government posts. Eisenhower won reelection in 1956 by a landslide, again over Stevenson.

Eisenhower, a moderate, won support from his own party and from many Southern Democrats. During his presidency, Congress extended Social Security benefits and passed the first civil rights act since Reconstruction. Despite his popularity, however, Eisenhower failed to make the Republican Party the country's majority party.

. . . Vice President Richard M. Nixon won the Republican presidential nomination in 1960, but he narrowly lost the election to his Democratic opponent, John F. Kennedy. Following Kennedy's assassination in 1963, Vice President Lyndon B. Johnson succeeded to the presidency. In 1964, the Republicans nominated Barry M. Goldwater, who stood for an extreme form of conservatism [at the time]. Johnson defeated him overwhelmingly. At Johnson's urging, Congress passed additional civil rights legislation and other laws to help disadvantaged Americans. Conservative

Republicans and conservative Southern Democrats joined forces to oppose many of Johnson's programs.

For the 1968 presidential election, the Republicans turned to Nixon again. The Democrats nominated Vice President Hubert H. Humphrey. A third party, the American Independent Party, nominated George C. Wallace, a Southern Democrat who strongly opposed civil rights legislation. Nixon won even though he received only 43 percent of the popular vote. He triumphed partly because of his "Southern strategy," in which he appealed to conservative white Southerners. Nixon emphasized patriotism and law and order. He favored slower school integration than liberals did.

In 1972, the Republicans renominated Nixon, and the Democrats nominated George S. McGovern. Nixon received over 17¾ million more popular votes than McGovern—the widest margin of any presidential election in U.S. history.

. . . In 1973, Nixon helped end U.S. involvement in the Vietnam War. But his administration suffered a loss of public confidence later that year, because of the Watergate scandal and another criminal investigation that led to the resignation of Vice President Spiro T. Agnew . . . House minority leader Gerald R. Ford replaced Agnew as vice president. In July 1974, the House Judiciary Committee recommended that Nixon be impeached on charges related to the Watergate scandal. Nixon resigned in August, before the House voted on impeachment, and Ford became president.

The Agnew and Watergate scandals damaged the Republican Party. By the mid-1970s, less than one-fourth of American voters called themselves Republicans. In 1976, the Republicans suffered a split within their party, as

Ronald Reagan, a conservative who had served as governor of California, challenged the more moderate Ford for the presidential nomination. Ford won the nomination but lost to Jimmy Carter, the Democratic candidate, for the general election.

. . . The Republicans won every presidential election in the 1980s. The party, strengthened by social conservatives who opposed abortion and supported school prayer, solidified the gains Nixon had made in the South. The party also continued to appeal to economic conservatives by supporting tax cuts and a balanced federal budget.

In 1980, Republicans chose Ronald Reagan as their presidential candidate. The Democrats renominated Carter, and Representative John B. Anderson of Illinois ran as an independent. Reagan won by a wide margin. The Republicans also won control of the Senate. In the 1984 presidential election, Reagan defeated his Democratic opponent, Walter F. Mondale. In the 1986 elections, the Democrats regained control of the Senate. In 1988, Vice President George H. W. Bush won the Republican presidential nomination. He went on to defeat his Democratic opponent, Michael S. Dukakis.

. . . In 1992, the Republicans renominated Bush for president. The Democrats nominated Arkansas Governor Bill Clinton, and Texas businessman Ross Perot ran as an independent. Bush and Perot lost the election to Clinton. In 1994, the Republicans won control of both houses of Congress. The party had not controlled both houses since 1955. In 1996, Senator Robert Dole of Kansas, the Republican nominee, lost the presidential election to Clinton. However, the Republicans retained control of both houses of Congress in 1996 and 1998.

. . . During the 2000 presidential primaries, divisions between moderate and conservative Republicans gained widespread attention. Arizona Senator John McCain, a moderate and a Vietnam War veteran, ran against Texas Governor George W. Bush, son of former President George H. W. Bush. Bush considered social conservatives his base of political support, especially in the South. He won the nomination and defeated the Democratic candidate, Vice President Al Gore, in a close election . . .

Bush was reelected in 2004, defeating Democratic Senator John F. Kerry of Massachusetts. During Bush's second term, however, the Republicans suffered from congressional scandals and from criticism over the administration's handling of the Iraq War (2003-2010). In 2006, Republicans lost control of both Houses of Congress to the Democrats.

In 2008, Democratic Senator Barack Obama of Illinois defeated John McCain, the Republican nominee. Obama became the nation's first African American president. [The Great Recession] struck in the months before the election [and] contributed to the Republican defeat.[8]

2010 was a year of political success for the GOP, starting with the upset win of Scott Brown in the Massachusetts special Senate election for the seat held for many decades by the Kennedy brothers. In the November elections, the GOP recaptured control of the House, increased their number of seats in the Senate, and gained a majority of governorships.

---

[8]   The World Book Encyclopedia, (Chicago, IL: World Book, Inc., 2012), Volume 16, pp. 253-257.

In state legislatures, Republicans gained 680 seats, the biggest gain by either party since 1966. After the elections, Republicans held approximately 3,890 of the total state legislative seats in the U.S.—about 53%, the most seats in the GOP column since 1928. The Republicans won control of at least 54 of the 99 state legislative chambers, the highest number since 1952.[9]

"Republican Party" from the *World Book Encyclopedia* © 2012 World Book, Inc. By permission of the publisher. www.worldbook.com. All rights reserved. This article may not be reproduced in whole or in part in any form without prior written permission from World Book, Inc.

---

[9]   See http://en.wikipedia.org/wiki/Republican_party_(United_States).

Chapter 3
Party Ideology

This chapter provides an overview of the ideologies behind each party in an effort to help you better understand what each one stands for. Such an understanding is instrumental in deciding which party to support. It is important to learn the specific positions taken by a given candidate before casting your vote. Note: Except for their respective introductory paragraphs, Chapters 3 and 4 are paraphrased from Wikipedia.org unless otherwise indicated. Articles were examined fully to eliminate potential inaccuracies.

DEMOCRATIC PARTY

Since the 1890s, the Democratic Party has favored socially liberal positions. In recent exit polls, it has had broad appeal across all socio-ethno-economic demographics. Historically, the party has favored farmers, laborers, labor unions, and religious and ethnic minorities; it has opposed unregulated business and finance, and favored progressive income taxes. In the 1930s, the party began advocating welfare spending programs targeted at the poor. It had a fiscally conservative, pro-business wing, typified by Grover Cleveland and Al Smith, and a Southern conservative wing that shrank after President Lyndon B. Johnson supported the Civil Rights Act of 1964. The major influences for liberalism were labor unions (which peaked in the 1936-to-1952 era) and the African-American wing, which has grown steadily since the 1960s. Since the 1970s, environmentalism has been a major new component.

Democrats generally support a more progressive tax structure to provide more services and reduce economic inequality. Currently, they have proposed allowing tax cuts given by the Bush administration to the wealthiest Americans to expire as written in the original legislation while keeping those given to the middle class in place. Democrats generally support more government spending on social services while spending less on the military. They oppose the cutting of social services such as Social Security, Medicare, Medicaid, and various welfare programs, believing it harmful to social justice and efficiency. Democrats believe that social services, in both monetary and non-monetary terms, result in a more productive labor force and believe that the benefits of this are greater than any benefits derived from lower taxes, especially on top earners, or cuts to social services. Furthermore, Democrats see social services as essential towards providing freedom derived from economic opportunity.

Democrats call for "affordable and quality health care," and many advocate an expansion of government intervention in this area. Many Democrats favor national health insurance or universal health care in a variety of forms to address the rising costs of modern health insurance. The Progressive Democrats of America, a group operating inside the Democratic Party, has made single-payer universal health care one of their primary policy goals.

Health insurance policies favored by most Democrats include:

- Ending the ability of insurers to drop coverage when people get sick;

- Ending insurance companies' ability to discriminate based on preexisting conditions;
- Ending lifetime caps on benefits and payments provided by insurers;
- Allowing children to stay on their parents' coverage until age 26;
- The expansion of Medicare to those aged 55;
- Closing the "donut hole" in Medicare Part D;
- Mandating coverage for all Americans;
- Expansion of Medicaid;
- Creating a nationwide insurance exchange across state lines;
- Dropping the current antitrust provision for insurance companies;
- Requiring large businesses to provide employer-based insurance;
- Providing subsidies for low to moderate-income families and small businesses; and
- Importing Canadian drugs and creating a national public insurance option paid for by premiums and co-pays.

Many of these proposals were included in the Patient Protection and Affordable Care Act and Health Care and Education Reconciliation Act of 2010. The Congressional Budget Office (CBO) estimates that the Affordable Care Act will reduce the national deficit by more than $100 billion over the next 10 years.[10]

The Democratic Party supports equal opportunity for all Americans regardless of sex, age, race, ethnicity, sexual orientation, gender identity, religion, creed, or national

---

[10] "The Ed Show," MSNBC, 3/26/2012.

origin. The party supports affirmative action programs to further this goal. Democrats also strongly support the Americans with Disabilities Act to prohibit discrimination against people based on physical or mental disability.

Most members of the Democratic Party believe that all women should have access to birth control, and support public funding of contraception for poor women. The party opposes attempts to reverse the 1973 Supreme Court decision on *Roe v. Wade*, which declared abortion covered by the constitutionally protected individual right to privacy under the Ninth Amendment, and *Planned Parenthood v. Casey*, which lays out the legal framework in which courts assess government actions that allegedly violate that right. Many Democrats consider a woman's ability to choose to abort without governmental interference a matter of her right to privacy and gender equality. They believe that each woman, conferring with her conscience, has the right to choose for herself whether abortion is morally correct.

The Democratic Party has been divided on the subject of same-sex marriage, though most of the support for same-sex marriage in the United States has come from Democrats. Some members favor civil unions for same-sex couples, others favor full and equal legalized marriage, and others are opposed to same-sex marriage on religious or ideological grounds. Support for same-sex marriage has increased in the past decade according to *ABC News*, with an April 2009 *ABC News/Washington Post* public opinion poll putting support among Democrats at 62%.[11] A broad majority of Democrats have supported other LGBT-related laws such as extending hate crime statutes, legally preventing

---

[11]   "Changing Views on Social Issues." 4/30/2009. Retrieved 5/14/2009.

discrimination against LGBT people in the workforce, and repealing Don't ask, Don't tell. A 2006 Pew Research Center poll of Democrats found that 55% support gays adopting children with 40% opposed while 70% support gays in the military with only 23% opposed.[12] Gallup polling from May 2009 stated that 82% of Democrats support open enlistment.[13]

Democrats have long believed that government should protect the environment. In more recent years, the party's environmental stance has emphasized alternative energy generation as the basis for an improved economy, greater national security, and general environmental benefits. The party also favors expansion of conservation lands and encourages open space and rail travel to relieve highway and airport congestion and improve air quality. Its most important environmental concern is global warming. Democrats, most notably former Vice-President Al Gore, have pressed for stern regulation of greenhouse gases. On October 15, 2007, Gore won the Nobel Peace Prize for his efforts to build greater knowledge about man-made climate change and lay the foundations for the measures needed to counteract these changes, asserting that "the climate crisis is not a political issue, it is a moral and spiritual challenge to all of humanity."[14]

---

[12] Less Opposition to Gay Marriage, Adoption and Military Service. Pew Research Center. Published 3/22/2006.

[13] Morales, Lymari (6/5/2009). "Conservatives Shift in Favor of Openly Gay Service Members." Gallup.com.

[14] John Nicols (2007-10-12). "Al Gore Wins Nobel Peace Prize." The Nation.

The Democratic Party believes that individuals should have a right to privacy. For example, Democrats have generally opposed the National Security Agency's (NSA's) warrantless surveillance of U.S. citizens. Some Democratic officeholders have championed consumer protection laws that limit the sharing of consumer data between corporations. Most Democrats oppose sodomy laws and believe that government should not regulate consensual noncommercial sexual conduct among adults as a matter of personal privacy.

Many Democrats are opposed to the use of torture against individuals apprehended and held prisoner by the U.S. military, and hold that categorizing such prisoners as unlawful combatants does not release the U.S. from its obligations under the Geneva Conventions. Democrats contend that torture is inhumane, decreases the United States' moral standing in the world, and produces questionable results. Democrats largely spoke out against waterboarding.

With a stated goal of reducing crime and homicide, the Democratic Party has introduced various gun control measures, most notably the Gun Control Act of 1968, the Brady Bill of 1993, and the Crime Control Act of 1994. However, some Democrats, especially rural, Southern, and Western Democrats, favor fewer restrictions on firearm possession and claim the party was defeated in the 2000 presidential election in rural areas over this issue. In the national platform for 2008, the only statement explicitly favoring gun control was a plan calling for renewal of the 1994 Assault Weapons Ban.

The Democratic Party lends far less support to the death penalty than the Republican Party. Though most

Democrats in Congress have never seriously moved to overturn the rarely used federal death penalty, both Russ Feingold and Dennis Kucinich have introduced such bills with little success. Democrats have led efforts to overturn state death penalty laws, particularly in New Jersey and in New Mexico. They have also sought to prevent reinstatement of the death penalty in states that currently prohibit it, including Massachusetts and New York. During the Clinton administration, Democrats led the expansion of the federal death penalty. These efforts resulted in the passage of the Antiterrorism and Effective Death Penalty Act of 1996. Signed into law by President Clinton, the law heavily limited appeals in death penalty cases.[15]

REPUBLICAN PARTY

The Republican Party's platform generally reflects American conservatism in the U.S. political spectrum. As of 2004, the party has remained fairly cohesive, as both strong economic libertarians and social conservatives oppose the Democrats, whom they see as a party of bloated and more secular, liberal government. Yet, some libertarians have argued that the GOP's policies have grown increasingly restrictive of personal liberties and have contributed to increasing corporate welfare and national debt. Some social conservatives have expressed dissatisfaction with the party's support for economic policies that they see as sometimes in conflict with their moral values.

Republicans emphasize the role of free markets and individual achievement as the primary factors behind economic prosperity. To this end, they favor laissez-faire

---

[15]   See http://en.wikipedia.org/wiki/Democratic_Party_(United_States).

economics, fiscal conservatism, and the promotion of personal responsibility over welfare programs.

A leading economic theory advocated by modern Republicans is supply-side economics. Some fiscal policies influenced by this theory were popularly known as Reaganomics, a term popularized during Ronald Reagan's terms in office. The theory holds that reduced income tax rates increase GDP growth and thereby generate the same or more revenue for the government from the smaller tax on the extra growth. This belief is reflected, in part, by the party's long-term advocacy of tax cuts. Many Republicans consider the income tax system to be inherently inefficient and oppose graduated tax rates, which they believe are unfairly targeted at those who create jobs and wealth. They believe private spending is usually more efficient than government spending. Republicans oppose the estate tax.

While most Republicans agree there should be a "safety net" to assist the less fortunate, they tend to believe the private sector is more effective than government in helping the poor. As a result, Republicans support giving government grants to faith-based and other private charitable organizations to supplant welfare spending. Members of the GOP also believe that limits on eligibility and benefits must be in place to ensure the safety net is not abused. Republicans introduced and strongly supported the 1996 Welfare Reform Act, which was signed into law by Democratic President Clinton. It limited eligibility for welfare, leading successfully to many former welfare recipients finding jobs.

The party opposes a government-run, single-payer health care system, believing such a system constitutes socialized medicine, and is in favor of a personal or employer-based system of insurance, supplemented by Medicare for the elderly and Medicaid, which covers approximately 40% of the poor. The GOP has a mixed record of supporting the historically popular Social Security, Medicare, and Medicaid programs. Congressional Republicans and the Bush administration supported a reduction in Medicaid's growth rate; however, congressional Republicans expanded Medicare, supporting a new drug plan for seniors starting in 2006.

In 2011, House Republicans overwhelmingly voted for a proposal named "The Path to Prosperity" and for major changes to Medicare, Medicaid, and the 2010 Health Care Legislation. For the most part, they oppose government funding for elective abortions.

Republicans are generally opposed by labor union management and members. They have supported right-to-work legislation at the state and federal levels as well as the Taft-Hartley Act, which gives workers the right not to participate in unions (as opposed to a closed shop, which prohibits workers from choosing not to join unions in workplaces). Some Republicans are opposed to increases in the minimum wage, believing that such increases hurt many businesses by forcing them to cut jobs and services, export jobs overseas, and raise the prices of goods to compensate for the decrease in profit.

Many contemporary Republicans have voiced support of strict constructionism, the judicial philosophy that the Constitution should be interpreted narrowly and as close to the original intent as is practicable, rather than as a more flexible "living Constitution" model. Most Republicans point to *Roe v. Wade* as a case of judicial activism wherein the court overturned most laws restricting abortion on the basis of a right to privacy inferred from the Bill of Rights and the 14th Amendment to the United States Constitution. Some Republicans have actively sought to block judges whom they see as activist and have instead sought the appointment of judges who claim to practice judicial restraint. The issue of judicial deference to the legislature is a matter of some debate—like the Democrats, most Republicans criticize court decisions that overturn their own (conservative) legislation as overstepping bounds and support decisions that overturn opposing legislation. Some commentators have advocated that the Republicans take a more aggressive approach and support legislative supremacy more firmly.

Within the last decade, the Republican Party has supported various bills to strip some or all federal courts of the ability to hear certain types of cases in an attempt to limit judicial review. Compared with Democrats, many Republicans believe in a more robust version of federalism with greater limitations placed upon federal power and a larger role reserved for the states.

In 2000, the Republican Party adopted as part of its platform support for the development of market-based solutions to environmental problems. According to the platform, "economic prosperity and environmental protection must advance together, environmental regulations should be based on science, the government's role should be to provide market-based incentives to develop the technologies to meet environmental standards, we should ensure that environmental policy meets the needs of localities, and environmental policy should focus on achieving results processes."[16] Some Republicans support increased oil drilling in currently protected areas such as the Arctic National Wildlife Refuge, a position that has drawn sharp criticism from some activists.

Republicans are generally against affirmative action for women and some minorities and often describe it as a quota system. They believe it is non-meritocratic and socially counter-productive in that it promotes further discrimination. Many Republicans support race-neutral admissions policies in universities but also support taking into account the socioeconomic status of the student.

Most of the GOP's membership favors capital punishment and stricter punishments as a means to prevent crime. Republicans generally support gun ownership rights and oppose laws regulating guns, although some Republicans in urban areas sometimes favor limited restrictions on the grounds that they are necessary to ensure safety in large cities.

Most Republicans support school choice through charter schools and school vouchers for private schools; many have denounced the performance of the public school system and the teachers' unions. The party has insisted on a system of greater accountability for public schools, most prominently in recent years with the No Child Left Behind Act of 2001. Many Republicans, however, opposed the creation of the United States Department of Education when it was initially established in 1979. Some in the religious wing of the party support voluntary organized prayer in public schools and the teaching of intelligent design in science classes.

---

[16] "Encourage Market-Based Solutions to Environmental Problems." OnTheIssues. 2000-08-12.

Although the GOP has voted for increases in government funding of scientific research, some members actively oppose the federal funding of embryonic stem cell research beyond the original lines because it involves the destruction of human embryos, which many consider ethically equivalent to abortion. At the same time, some members argue for the application of research money into adult stem cell or amniotic stem cell research. The stem cell issue has garnered two once-rare vetoes on research funding bills from President Bush, who said the research was morally unacceptable. A majority of the GOP's national and state candidates are pro-life and oppose elective abortion on religious or moral grounds.

The 2004 Republican platform expressed support for the Federal Marriage Amendment to the United States Constitution to define marriage as exclusively between one man and one woman. Generally speaking, most Republicans have opposed government recognition of same-sex unions such as same-sex marriage. This opposition formed a key method of energizing conservative voters, the Republican base, in the 2004 election. Historically, most Republicans have opposed permitting LGBT people to serve openly in the military and supported Don't ask, Don't tell. However, according to Gallup polling, majorities of 52% and 58% among Republicans in both 2004 and 2009 respectively opposed the policy and supported open enlistment.[17] Groups pushing for LGBT issues inside the party include the Log Cabin Republicans and GOProud.

Some in the Republican Party support unilateralism on issues of national security, believing in the ability and

---

[17]   Morales, Lymari (June 5, 2009). "Conservatives Shift in Favor of Openly Gay Service Members." Gallup.

right of the United States to act without external support in matters of national defense. In general, Republican thinking on defense and international relations is heavily influenced by the theories of neorealism and realism, characterizing conflicts between nations as struggles between faceless forces of international structure as opposed to the result of the ideas and actions of individual leaders. The realist school's influence can be seen in Ronald Reagan's Evil Empire stance on the Soviet Union and George W. Bush's "axis of evil" definition.

Republicans secured gains in the 2002 and 2004 elections, with the War on Terror one of the top issues in their favor. Since the attacks of September 11, 2001, some in the party have supported neoconservative policies with regard to the War on Terror, including the 2001 war in Afghanistan and the 2003 invasion of Iraq. The doctrine of preemptive war—wars fought to disarm and destroy potential military foes based on speculation of future attacks rather than in defense against actual attacks—has been advocated by prominent members of the Bush administration, but the war in Iraq has undercut the influence of this doctrine within the Republican Party.

The George W. Bush administration took the position that the Geneva Conventions do not apply to unlawful combatants, only to soldiers serving in the armies of nation states and not terrorist organizations such as al-Qaeda. The Supreme Court overruled this position in *Hamdan v. Rumsfeld*, which held that the Geneva Conventions were legally binding and must be followed in regards to all enemy combatants. Prominent Republicans such as John McCain, Mike Huckabee, and Ron Paul strongly oppose the use of enhanced interrogation techniques, which they view as torture.

Through former U.N. Ambassador John Bolton, the Republican Party has advocated reforms in the United Nations to halt corruption such as that which afflicted the Oil-for-Food Programme. Most Republicans oppose the Kyoto Protocol. The party promotes free trade agreements, most notably the North American Free Trade Agreement and the Dominican Republic-Central America Free Trade Agreement. Some Republicans have promoted free trade further south in Brazil, Peru, and Colombia, although some hold a protectionist view in that regard.

Republicans are divided on how to confront illegal immigration between a platform that allows for migrant workers and easing citizenship guidelines and one that advocates a border-enforcement-first approach. In general, pro-growth advocates within the Republican Party support more immigration, and traditional or populist conservatives oppose it. In 2006, the White House supported and the Republican-led Senate passed comprehensive immigration reform that would eventually allow millions of illegal immigrants to become citizens. However, the House, also led by Republicans, took an enforcement-first approach, and the bill failed to pass the conference committee.[18]

---

[18]   See http://en.wikipedia.org/wiki/Republican_party_(United_States).

CHAPTER 4
SAMPLE LEGISLATION

This chapter details select landmark legislation enacted by Congress from 1919 until 2010, beginning with the very first act made into law. Each piece of legislation is presented by date in abridged format to facilitate reading. The name of each law is highlighted in **bold**.

An Act to regulate the Time and Manner of administering certain Oaths was the first law passed by the Congress assembled after the ratification of the U.S. Constitution. President George Washington signed it on June 1, 1789, and parts of it remain in effect to this day.

The House of Representatives reached its first quorum on April 1, 1789. Five days later, it appointed a committee to draft a bill on the manner of administration of the oath for members of Congress required under Article VI of the Constitution. On April 25, 1789, the committee reported its bill to the whole House, which approved it two days later. The Senate committee charged with the bill added a section requiring state officials and legislators to take the same oath as members of Congress. The Senate approved the bill with the change on May 5. The House did not object to the Senate's change, and representatives of each body took the bill to President Washington for his signature.[19]

---

[19]   See http://en.wikipedia.org/wiki/An_act_to_regulate_the_time_and_manner_of_administering_certain_oaths.

The **National Prohibition Act**, known informally as the **Volstead Act** (enacted October 18, 1919), was the enabling legislation for the 18th Amendment, which established Prohibition in the United States. The bill was named for Andrew Volstead, Chairman of the House Judiciary Committee, who managed the legislation. It passed the House by an overwhelming margin of 230 to 69 and passed the Senate by a voice vote. It was subsequently vetoed by President Woodrow Wilson on October 27, 1919. The veto was overridden by the House 175 to 55, and overridden by the Senate 65 to 20.

The three distinct purposes of the act were to:

1. Prohibit intoxicating beverages;
2. Regulate the manufacture, sale, or transport of intoxicating liquor; and
3. Ensure an ample supply of alcohol and promote its use in scientific research and in the development of fuel, dye, and other lawful industries and practices, such as religious rituals.

It provided further that no person should manufacture, sell, barter, transport, import, export, deliver, or furnish any intoxicating liquor except as authorized by the act.

The effects of prohibition were largely unanticipated. Production, importation, and distribution of alcoholic beverages—once the province of legitimate businesses—were taken over by criminal gangs, which fought each other for market control in violent confrontations, including mass murder. Major gangsters, such as Omaha's Tom Dennison and Chicago's Al Capone, became rich in the process. Enforcement was difficult because the gangs became so rich they were often able to bribe underpaid and understaffed law-enforcement personnel and pay for expensive lawyers.

Many respectable citizens were sympathetic to bootleggers and lured by the romance of illegal speakeasies. The loosening of social mores during the 1920s resulted in the popularization of the cocktail and the cocktail party among higher socioeconomic groups. Those inclined to help authorities were often intimidated and even murdered. In several major cities—notably those serving as major points of liquor importation (including Chicago and Detroit)—gangs wielded significant political power.

The act called for trials for anyone charged with an alcohol-related offense, and juries often failed to convict. Prohibition led to disrespect for the law and the growth of organized crime and lost advocates as alcohol gained increasing social acceptance. By 1933, public opposition to prohibition had become overwhelming. Congress passed the Blaine Act, a proposed constitutional amendment to repeal prohibition, in February. On December 5, 1933, Utah became the 36th state to ratify the 21st Amendment, which repealed the 18th Amendment, rendered the Volstead Act unconstitutional, and restored control of alcohol to the states. The creation of the Federal Alcohol Administration in 1935 defined a modest role for the federal government with respect to alcohol and its taxation.[20]

The Blaine Act was sponsored by Wisconsin Senator John J. Blaine and passed by the United States Senate on February 17, 1933. It initiated the repeal of the 18th Amendment to the United States Constitution, which established prohibition in the United States. The repeal was

---

[20]   See http://en.wikipedia.org/wiki/National_Prohibition_Act.

formally adopted as the 21st Amendment to the Constitution on December 5, 1933.[21]

The 21st Amendment contains three sections that read as follows:

- Section 1: The eighteenth article of amendment to the Constitution of the United States is hereby repealed.
- Section 2: The transportation or importation into any State, Territory, or possession of the United States for delivery or use therein of intoxicating liquors, in violation of the laws thereof, is hereby prohibited.
- Section 3: This article shall be inoperative unless it shall have been ratified as an amendment to the Constitution by conventions in the several States, as provided in the Constitution, within seven years from the date of the submission hereof to the States by the Congress.

The Congress proposed the 21st Amendment on February 20, 1933, and the amendment was adopted on December 5, 1933. It is the only amendment to have been ratified by state ratifying conventions, specially selected for the purpose. All other amendments have been ratified by state legislatures. It is also the only amendment approved for the explicit purpose of repealing a previously existing amendment to the Constitution. The 21st Amendment ending national prohibition officially took effect on

---

[21] See http://en.wikipedia.org/wiki/Blaine_Act.

December 15, though people started drinking openly before that date.[22]

The Banking Act of 1933 (enacted June 16, 1933) was a law that established the Federal Deposit Insurance Corporation (FDIC) in the United States and imposed banking reforms, several of which were intended to control speculation. It is often referred to as the **Glass-Steagall Act** after its congressional sponsors, Senator Carter Glass (D) of Virginia and Representative Henry B. Steagall (D) of Alabama. It passed the House by an overwhelming margin of 262 to 19, and passed the Senate by a voice vote.

The term "Glass-Steagall Act," however, is most often used to refer to four provisions of the Banking Act of 1933 that limited commercial bank securities activities and affiliations between commercial banks and securities firms. Starting in the early 1960s, federal banking regulators interpreted these provisions as permitting commercial banks and especially commercial bank affiliates to engage in an expanding list and volume of securities activities. By the time the affiliation restrictions in the Glass-Steagall Act were repealed through the Gramm-Leach-Bliley Act in 1999, many commentators argued Glass-Steagall was already "dead."

Many commentators have stated that the Gramm-Leach-Bliley Act's repeal of the affiliation restrictions of the Glass-Steagall Act was an important cause of the late-2000s financial crisis. Others have argued that the activities linked to the financial crisis were not prohibited (or, in most cases, even regulated) by the

---

[22]   See http://en.wikipedia.org/wiki/
Twenty-first_Amendment_to_the_United_States_Constitution.

Glass-Steagall Act. Commentators have also argued that the ability of commercial banking firms to acquire securities firms (and of securities firms to convert into bank holding companies) helped mitigate the financial crisis. This repeal directly contributed to the severity of the financial crisis of 2007 to 2011 by allowing Wall Street investment banking firms to gamble with their depositors' money held in the commercial banks.[23]

The Civil Rights Act of 1957, primarily a voting rights bill, was the first civil rights legislation enacted by Congress in the United States since Reconstruction following the American Civil War. It set out to enforce the voting rights of African Americans as set out in the 15th Amendment of the United States Constitution.

Senator Strom Thurmond of South Carolina, an ardent segregationist, sustained the longest one-person filibuster in history (24 hours and 18 minutes) in an attempt to keep the bill from becoming law. The bill passed the House with a vote of 270 to 97 and the Senate 60 to 15. President Eisenhower signed it into law on September 9, 1957.

Following the historic U.S. Supreme Court ruling in *Brown v. Board of Education* (1955), which eventually led to the integration of public schools, Southern whites in Virginia began a "Massive Resistance." Violence against blacks rose there and elsewhere, as in Little Rock, Arkansas, where that year President Dwight D. Eisenhower ordered federal troops to protect nine children integrating into a public school, the first time the federal government had sent troops to the South since Reconstruction. The South saw continued physical assaults against suspected activists

---

23   See http://en.wikipedia.org/wiki/Glass%E2%80%93Steagall_Act.

and bombings of schools and churches. The Eisenhower administration proposed legislation to protect the right to vote by African Americans.

The goal of the 1957 Civil Rights Act was to ensure that all Americans could exercise their right to vote. By 1957, only about 20% of African Americans were registered to vote. Despite comprising the majority population in numerous counties and congressional districts in the South, discriminatory voter registration rules and laws had effectively disfranchised most blacks in those states since the late-19th and early-20th centuries. Civil rights organizations had collected evidence of discriminatory practices, such as the administration of literacy and comprehension tests, poll taxes, and other means. While the states had the right to establish rules for voter registration and elections, the federal government took an oversight role in ensuring that citizens could exercise the constitutional right to vote for federal officers such as the president, vice-president, and members of Congress.

Democratic Senate Majority Leader Lyndon Baines Johnson from Texas realized that the bill and its journey through Congress could tear apart his party, whose Southern bloc was anti-civil rights and Northern members were more pro-civil rights. Johnson sent the bill to the judiciary committee, led by Senator James Eastland from Mississippi, who proceeded to change and alter the bill almost beyond recognition. Senator Richard Russell from Georgia had claimed the bill an example of the federal government's desire to impose its laws on the states. Johnson sought recognition from civil rights advocates for passage of the bill. while also receiving recognition from the mostly Southern anti-civil rights Democrats for reducing it so much as to kill it.

Although passage of the Civil Rights Act of 1957 seemed to indicate a growing federal commitment to the cause of civil rights, the legislation was limited. Due to the changes imposed on the act, the government had difficulty enforcing it, and by 1960, black voting had only increased 3%.[24]

The Civil Rights Act of 1960 (enacted May 6, 1960) was a United States federal law that established federal inspection of local voter registration rolls and introduced penalties for anyone who obstructed another's attempt to vote or to register to vote. It was designed to deal with discriminatory laws and practices in the segregated South, by which blacks had been effectively disfranchised since the late-19th and early-20th centuries. It extended the life of the Civil Rights Commission, previously limited to two years, to oversee registration and voting practices. The act was signed into law by President Dwight D. Eisenhower and served to eliminate certain loopholes left by the Civil Rights Act of 1957. It passed the House by an overwhelming margin of 311 to 109 and passed the Senate 71 to 18.[25]

The Civil Rights Act of 1964 (enacted July 2, 1964) was a landmark piece of legislation in the United States that outlawed major forms of discrimination against African Americans and women, including racial segregation. It ended unequal application of voter registration requirements and racial segregation in schools, at the workplace, and by facilities that served the general public ("public accommodations").

---

24 See http://en.wikipedia.org/wiki/Civil_Rights_Act_of_1957.

25 See http://en.wikipedia.org/wiki/Civil_Rights_Act_of_1960.

Powers given to enforce the act were initially weak, but were supplemented during later years. Congress asserted its authority to legislate under several different parts of the United States Constitution, principally its power to regulate interstate commerce under Article One (Section 8), its duty to guarantee all citizens equal protection of the laws under the 14th Amendment, and its duty to protect voting rights under the 15th Amendment. The act was signed into law by President Lyndon B. Johnson, who would later sign the landmark Voting Rights Act into law. It passed the House by a margin of 290 to 130, and passed the Senate 71 to 29.

The bill divided and engendered a long-term change in the demographics of both parties. President Johnson realized that supporting it would risk losing the South's overwhelming support of the Democratic Party. Both Attorney General Robert Kennedy and Vice-President Johnson had pushed for the introduction of the legislation. Johnson told Kennedy aide Ted Sorensen, "I know the risks are great and we might lose the South, but those sorts of states may be lost anyway."[26] Senator Richard Russell, Jr. warned President Johnson about his strong support for the civil rights bill: "[It] will not only cost you the South, it will cost you the election."[27] Johnson, however, went on to win the 1964 election by one of the biggest landslides in American history.

The South, which had been voting Republican increasingly since the 1930s, continued the trend, and by

---

[26] Kotz, Nick (2005), Judgment Days: Lyndon Baines Johnson, Martin Luther King, Jr., and the Laws that Changed America, p. 61.

[27] Branch, Taylor (1998), Pillar of Fire, p. 187.

the 1990s had become the stronghold of the Republican Party. Although majorities in both parties voted for the bill, there were notable exceptions. Republican Senator Barry Goldwater of Arizona voted against the bill, declaring morality cannot be legislated.

The constitutionality of the Civil Rights Act of 1964 was, at the time, in some dispute as it applied to the private sector. The United States Supreme Court had ruled in landmark civil rights cases that Congress did not have the power to prohibit discrimination in the private sector, thus stripping the Civil Rights Act of 1875 of much of its ability to protect civil rights. Even today, the Supreme Court has struck down parts of civil rights laws on the grounds that the 14th Amendment does not give Congress the power to prohibit private sector discrimination. In the late-19th and early-20th centuries, the legal justification for voiding the Civil Rights Act of 1875 was part of a larger trend by members of the United States Supreme Court to invalidate most government regulations of the private sector, except when dealing with laws designed to protect traditional public morality.

In the 1930s, during the New Deal, the majority of the Supreme Court justices gradually shifted their legal theory to allow for greater government regulation of the private sector under the commerce clause, thereby paving the way for the federal government to enact civil rights laws prohibiting both public—and private-sector discrimination. After the Civil Rights Act of 1964 was passed, the Supreme Court upheld the law's application to the private sector on the grounds that Congress had the power to regulate commerce between the states.[28]

The Voting Rights Act of 1965 (enacted August 6, 1965) is a landmark piece of national legislation in the United States that outlawed the discriminatory voting practices responsible for the widespread disenfranchisement of African Americans in the United States.

Echoing the language of the 15th Amendment, the act prohibits states from imposing any "voting qualification or prerequisite to voting, or standard, practice, or procedure . . . to deny or abridge the right of any citizen of the United States to vote on account of race or color."[29] Specifically, Congress intended the act to outlaw the practice of requiring otherwise qualified voters to pass literacy tests in order to register to vote, a principal means by which Southern states had prevented African Americans from exercising the franchise. The act was signed into law by Democratic President Lyndon B. Johnson, who had earlier signed the landmark Civil Rights Act of 1964 into law. It passed the House by an overwhelming margin of 328 to 74, and passed the Senate 79 to 18.

The act is widely considered a landmark in civil rights legislation, though some of its provisions have sparked political controversy. During the debate over the 2006 extension, some Republican members of Congress objected to renewing the preclearance requirement (the act's primary enforcement provision), arguing that it represents an overreach of federal power and places unwarranted

---

[28] See http://en.wikipedia.org/wiki/Civil_Rights_Act_of_1964.

[29] "The Voting Rights Act of 1965." U.S. National Archives. Retrieved 2008-08-29.

bureaucratic demands on Southern states that have long since abandoned the discriminatory practices the act was meant to eradicate. Conservative legislators also opposed requiring states with large Spanish-speaking populations to provide bilingual ballots. Congress nonetheless voted to extend the act for 25 years with its original enforcement provisions left intact.[30]

The Civil Rights Act of 1968, also known as the Indian Civil Rights Act of 1968, (enacted April 11, 1968) was a landmark piece of legislation in the United States that provided for equal housing opportunities regardless of race, creed, or national origin. The act was signed into law by President Lyndon B. Johnson, who had previously signed the landmark Civil Rights Act and Voting Rights Act into law. It passed the House by an overwhelming margin of 326 to 93, and passed the Senate 71 to 20.

Title VIII of the Civil Rights Act of 1968 is commonly known as the Fair Housing Act and was meant as a follow-up to the Civil Rights Act of 1964. While the Civil Rights Act of 1866 prohibited discrimination in housing, there were no federal enforcement provisions. The 1968 act expanded on previous acts and prohibited discrimination concerning the sale, rental, and financing of housing based on race, religion, national origin, and, since 1974, gender. Since 1988, the act has protected people with disabilities and families with children.

Victims of discrimination may use both the 1968 act and the 1866 act via Section 1,983 to seek redress. The 1968 act provides for federal solutions while the 1866 act provides for private solutions (i.e., civil suits). A rider attached to the

---

[30]   See http://en.wikipedia.org/wiki/Voting_Rights_Act_of_1965.

bill makes it a felony to "travel in interstate commerce . . . with the intent to incite, promote, encourage, participate in and carry on a riot." This provision has been criticized for "equating organized political protest with organized violence."[31]

The Civil Rights Act of 1968 prohibited the following forms of discrimination:

1. Refusal to sell or rent a dwelling to any person because of his/her race, color, religion, or national origin. People with disabilities and families with children were added to the list of protected classes by the Fair Housing Amendments Act of 1988.
2. Discrimination against a person in the terms, conditions, or privilege of the sale or rental of a dwelling.
3. Advertising the sale or rental of a dwelling indicating preference of discrimination based on race, color, religion, or national origin (amended by Congress as part of the Housing and Community Development Act of 1974 to include sex and, as of 1988, people with disabilities and families with children.)
4. Coercing, threatening, intimidating, or interfering with a person's enjoyment or exercise of housing rights based on discriminatory reasons or retaliating against a person or organization that aids or encourages the exercise or enjoyment of fair housing rights.

---

[31] See http://www.nybooks.com/articles/archives/1969/jun/19/the-committee-to-defend-the-conspiracy.

In 1988, Congress voted to weaken the ability of plaintiffs to prosecute cases of discriminatory treatment in housing. However, the Fair Housing Act was also amended in 1988 to allow plaintiffs' attorneys to recover attorney's fees. The 1988 amendment also added people with disabilities and families with children to the classes covered by the act.[32]

The Civil Rights Act of 1991 (enacted November 21, 1991) is a United States statute that was passed in response to a series of United States Supreme Court decisions that limited the rights of employees who had sued their employers for discrimination. The act represented the first effort since the passage of the Civil Rights Act of 1964 to modify some of the basic procedural and substantive rights provided by federal law in employment discrimination cases. It provided for the right to trial by jury on discrimination claims and introduced the possibility of emotional distress damages, while limiting the amount that a jury could award. It passed the House by an overwhelming margin of 381 to 38, and passed the Senate 93 to 5.[33]

The Personal Responsibility and Work Opportunity Reconciliation Act of 1996 (PRWORA) is a United States federal law considered to mark a fundamental shift in both the method and goal of federal cash assistance to the poor. The bill added a workforce development component to welfare legislation, encouraging employment among the poor. Other changes to the welfare system included stricter conditions for food stamps eligibility, reductions in immigrant welfare assistance, and recipient

---

[32]   See http://en.wikipedia.org/wiki/Civil_Rights_Act_of_1968.

[33]   See http://en.wikipedia.org/wiki/Civil_Rights_Act_of_1991.

work requirements. The bill was a cornerstone of the Republican Contract with America and was introduced by Representative E. Clay Shaw, Jr., who believed welfare was partly responsible for bringing immigrants to the United States. President Bill Clinton signed the PRWORA into law on August 22, 1996, fulfilling his 1992 campaign promise to "end welfare as we have come to know it."[34] It passed the House by a margin of 256 to 170, and passed the Senate 74 to 24.

The PRWORA instituted Temporary Assistance for Needy Families (TANF), which became effective on July 1, 1997. TANF placed time limits on welfare assistance and replaced the Aid to Families with Dependent Children (AFDC) program, which had been in effect since 1935, and supplanted the Job Opportunities and Basic Skills Training (JOBS) program of 1988. The U.S. Chamber of Commerce heralded the law as a reassertion of America's work ethic, largely in response to the bill's workfare component. TANF was reauthorized in the Deficit Reduction Act of 2005.

In the 1980s, AFDC came under increasing bipartisan criticism for the program's alleged ineffectiveness. While acknowledging the need for a social safety net, Democrats often invoked the "culture of poverty" argument. Proponents of the bill argued that welfare recipients were "trapped in a cycle of poverty."[35] Highlighting instances of welfare fraud,

---

[34]   Clinton, Bill (October 23, 1991). "The New Covenant: Responsibility and Rebuilding the American Community. Remarks to Students at Georgetown University." Democratic Leadership Council. Retrieved 2010-04-20.

[35]   Gilliam, Franklin (1999). "The 'Welfare Queen' Experiment: How Viewers React to Images of African-American Mothers on Welfare"

conservatives often referred to the system as a welfare trap and pledged to dismantle the welfare state.

Republican governor Tommy Thompson began instituting welfare reform in Wisconsin during his governorship in the late 1980s and early 1990s. In lobbying the federal government to grant states wider latitude for implementing welfare, Thompson wanted a system where "pregnant teen-aged girls from Milwaukee, no matter what their background is or where they live, can pursue careers and chase their dreams."[36] His solution was workfare, whereby poor individuals, typically single mothers with children, had to work to receive assistance.

Passage of the PRWORA was the culmination of many years of debate in which the merits and flaws of AFDC were argued. Both sides used research to make their points, with each side often using the same piece of research to support the opposite view. The political atmosphere at the time of the PRWORA's passage included a Republican-controlled House of Representatives and Senate (defined by their Contract with America) and a Democratic president.

The PRWORA proposed TANF as AFDC's replacement. The congressional findings in the PRWORA highlighted dependency, out-of-wedlock birth, and intergenerational poverty as the main contributors to a faulty system. In instituting a block grant program, the PRWORA granted states the ability to design their own systems as long as they

---

(PDF). Nieman Reports (UCLA: Center for Communications and Community) 53 (2). Retrieved 2008-04-03.

[36] Thompson, Tommy; Bennett, William. "The Good News About Welfare Reform: Wisconsin's Success Story." Retrieved 2008-04-03.

met a set of basic federal requirements. The bill's primary requirements and effects included the following:

- Ending welfare as an entitlement program;
- Requiring recipients to begin working after two years of receiving benefits;
- Placing a lifetime limit of five years on benefits paid by federal funds;
- Aiming to encourage two-parent families and discouraging out-of-wedlock births; and
- Enhancing enforcement of child support.

The legislation also greatly limited funds available for unmarried parents under 18 and restricted any funding to immigrants (legal or illegal). Welfare and poverty rates both declined during the late 1990s, leading many commentators to declare the legislation a success. Between 1997 and 2000, enormous numbers of poor left or were terminated from the program, with a national drop of 53% in total recipients.[37]

The Gramm-Leach-Bliley Act (GLB), also known as the Financial Services Modernization Act of 1999 (enacted November 12, 1999) or the Citigroup Relief Act, was passed by the 106th United States Congress (1999 to 2001). It repealed part of the Glass-Steagall Act of 1933, removing barriers in the market among banking companies, securities companies, and insurance companies that prohibited any one institution from acting as any combination of an investment bank, a commercial bank, and an insurance company. With the passage of the Gramm-Leach-Bliley Act, commercial banks, investment banks, securities firms, and insurance companies were allowed to consolidate. The

---

[37]   See http://en.wikipedia.org/wiki/
Personal_Responsibility_and_Work_Opportunity_Act.

legislation was signed into law by President Bill Clinton. It passed the House by a margin of 241 to 132, and passed the Senate 54 to 44.

In February 2009, one of the act's co-authors, former Senator Phil Gramm, defended his bill:

> [I]f GLB was the problem, the crisis would have been expected to have originated in Europe where they never had Glass-Steagall requirements to begin with. Also, the financial firms that failed in this crisis, like Lehman, were the least diversified and the ones that survived, like J.P. Morgan, were the most diversified. Moreover, GLB didn't deregulate anything. It established the Federal Reserve as a super-regulator, overseeing all Financial Services Holding Companies. All activities of financial institutions continued to be regulated on a functional basis by the regulators that had regulated those activities prior to GLB.[38]

Many believe the act contributed directly to the 2007 subprime mortgage financial crisis. President Barack Obama has stated that GLB led to deregulation that, among other things, allowed for the creation of giant financial supermarkets that could own investment banks, commercial banks, and insurance firms, practices banned since the Great Depression. Its passage, critics also say, cleared the way for companies that were too big and intertwined to fail. Economists Robert Ekelund and Mark Thornton have also criticized the act for contributing to the

---

[38] Phil Gramm, "Deregulation and the Financial Panic", opinion pages of The Wall Street Journal, published and retrieved on February 20, 2009.

crisis, stating that "in a world regulated by a gold standard, 100% reserve banking, and no FDIC deposit insurance" the Financial Services Modernization Act would have made "perfect sense" as a legitimate act of deregulation, but under the present fiat monetary system it amounted to "corporate welfare for financial institutions and a moral hazard that will make taxpayers pay dearly."[39]

Nobel Prize-winning economist Joseph Stiglitz has also argued that the act helped to create the crisis. An article in liberal publication *The Nation* asserted that GLB was responsible for the creation of entities that took on more risk due to their being considered "too big to fail."[40],[41]

The Iraq Resolution or the **Iraq War Resolution** (formally the Authorization for Use of Military Force Against Iraq Resolution of 2002, enacted October 16, 2002) is a joint resolution passed by the United States Congress in October 2002, authorizing military action against Iraq. It passed the House by a margin of 297 to 133, and passed the Senate 77 to 23.

The resolution cited many factors to justify the use of military force against Iraq, including the following:

---

[39]   Ekelund, Robert; Thornton, Mark (2008-09-04). "More Awful Truths About Republicans" Ludwig von Mises Institute. Retrieved 2008-09-07.

[40]   Summer, Mark -- John McCain: Crisis Enabler. The Nation. September 21, 2008.

[41]   See http://en.wikipedia.org/wiki/ Gramm-Leach-Bliley_Financial_Services_Modernization_Act.

- Iraq's noncompliance with the conditions of the 1991 ceasefire agreement, including interference with U.N. weapons inspectors;
- Iraq's alleged weapons of mass destruction, and programs to develop such weapons, posed a "threat to the national security of the United States and international peace and security in the Persian Gulf region";
- Iraq's "capability and willingness to use weapons of mass destruction against other nations and its own people";
- Iraq's "brutal repression of its civilian population";
- Iraq's hostility towards the United States as demonstrated by the 1993 assassination attempt on former President George H. W. Bush and firing on coalition aircraft enforcing the no-fly zones following the 1991 Gulf War;
- The knowledge that members of al-Qaeda, an organization bearing responsibility for attacks on the United States, its citizens, and interests, including the attacks that occurred on September 11, 2001, are in Iraq;
- Iraq's continuing tendency to "aid and harbor other international terrorist organizations," including anti-United States terrorist organizations;
- The paying of bounties by Iraq to families of suicide bombers;
- The efforts by Congress and the president to fight terrorists and those who aided or harbored them;
- The authorization by the Constitution and the Congress for the resident to fight anti-United States terrorism; and

- The Turkey, Kuwait, and Saudi Arabia governments' fear of Saddam and desire to remove him from power.[42],[43]

Citing the Iraq Liberation Act of 1998, the resolution reiterated that it should be the policy of the United States to remove the Saddam Hussein regime and promote a democratic replacement.

Two of the 12 reasons within the Authorization for Use of Military Force Against Iraq Resolution of 2002 for invading Iraq—the capability to produce and/or the possession of weapons of mass destruction (WMD) and active links to al-Qaeda—have been challenged. The Bush administration asserted that two small trailers found in Iraq were "weapons factories," despite U.S. intelligence officials possessing evidence to the contrary. Weapon inspectors were given access to the alleged weapons factories, despite statements to the contrary by the Bush administration. Continuing these inspections was made impossible by the U.S.-led invasion of Iraq, which forced the U.N. inspectors out, their requests for more time ignored.

A 2007 report by the Inspector General of the Department of Defense, declassified and released at the request of Senator Carl M. Levin of Michigan (D), asserted that the claims of an operational working relationship between Iraq and al-Qaeda, as put forth by a key Pentagon office in the lead-up to the invasion of Iraq, were based on dubious or unconfirmed reports. Since the invasion

---

[42] "President, House Leadership Agree on Iraq Resolution" (Press release). The White House. 2002-10-02.

[43] "Joint Resolution to Authorize the Use of United States Armed Forces Against Iraq" (Press release). The White House. 2002-10-02.

of Iraq, President Bush has explicitly stated that Iraq was not involved in 9/11, which has also been concluded by subsequent reports, and that al-Qaeda were operating in areas outside of Saddam Hussein's control. In addition, the day before she voted on the resolution, Senator Hillary Rodham Clinton said during a speech on the Senate floor that there was no dispute that Hussein was not involved in the September 11th attacks.[44] Nevertheless, members of the administration have made repeated suggestive statements over the years with a message implying a link between Saddam Hussein and the attacks.

Skeptics argue that the administration knowingly distorted intelligence reports or ignored contrary information in constructing their case for the war. The Downing Street memo and the Bush-Blair memo are used to substantiate that allegation. Congressional Democrats sponsored both a request for documents and a resolution of inquiry.[45]

The Partial-Birth Abortion Ban Act of 2003 (enacted November 5, 2003) is a United States law prohibiting a form of late-term abortion that the act calls "partial-birth abortion," often referred to in medical literature as intact dilation and extraction. Under this law, "any physician who, in or affecting interstate or foreign commerce, knowingly

---

[44] 10/10/2002. Retrieved 7/1/2011. "Now, I believe the facts that have brought us to this fateful vote are not in doubt. [...] He has also given aid, comfort, and sanctuary to terrorists, including Al Qaeda members, though there is apparently no evidence of his involvement in the terrible events of September 11, 2001. [...] Now this much is undisputed."

[45] See http://en.wikipedia.org/wiki/ Authorization_for_Use_of_Military_Force_Against_Iraq.

performs a partial-birth abortion and thereby kills a human fetus shall be fined under this title or imprisoned not more than 2 years, or both." The law was enacted in 2003, and in 2007 its constitutionality was upheld by the U.S. Supreme Court in the case of *Gonzales v. Carhart*. It passed the House by a margin of 282 to 139, and passed the Senate 64 to 33.

The procedure described in the statute is usually performed in the second trimester, from 15 to 26 weeks, some of which occur before and some of which occur after viability. The law itself contains no reference to gestational age or viability. The present statute is directed only at a *method* of abortion, rather than at preventing any woman from obtaining an abortion.

The statute includes two findings of Congress:

1. A moral, medical, and ethical consensus exists that the practice of performing a partial-birth abortion . . . is a gruesome and inhumane procedure that is never medically necessary and should be prohibited.
2. Rather than being an abortion procedure that is embraced by the medical community, particularly among physicians who routinely perform other abortion procedures, partial-birth abortion remains a disfavored procedure that is not only unnecessary to preserve the health of the mother, but in fact poses serious risks to the long-term health of women and in some circumstances, their lives. As a result, at least 27 States banned the procedure as did the United States Congress which voted to ban the procedure during the 104th, 105th, and 106th Congresses.

Despite its finding that partial-birth abortion is "unnecessary to preserve the health of the mother," the statute includes the following provision:

A defendant accused of an offense under this section may seek a hearing before the State Medical Board on whether the physician's conduct was necessary to save the life of the mother whose life was endangered by a physical disorder, physical illness, or physical injury, including a life-endangering physical condition caused by or arising from the pregnancy itself.

Pro-choice groups object to this statute primarily because there is no exemption if the health of a woman is at risk. The constitutionality of the law was challenged immediately after the signing. Three different U.S. district courts declared the law unconstitutional. All three cited the law's omission of an exception for the health of the woman (as opposed to the life of the woman), and all three decisions cited precedents set by *Roe v. Wade* (1973) and *Stenberg v. Carhart* (2000), a case in which the Supreme Court struck down a state ban on "partial-birth abortion" as unconstitutional.

On April 18, 2007 the Supreme Court, in a 5-to-4 decision on *Gonzales v. Carhart,* held that the statute does not violate the Constitution. Justice Anthony Kennedy's majority opinion argued that the case differed from *Stenberg v. Carhart* in that the Partial Birth Abortion Act defined the banned procedure more clearly. In dissent, Ginsburg argued that the decision departed from established abortion jurisprudence, and that lack of a health exception jeopardized women's health and placed doctors in a difficult position.[46]

---

[46]   See http://en.wikipedia.org/wiki/Partial-Birth_Abortion_Ban_Act.

The Lilly Ledbetter Fair Pay Act is a United States federal statute and the first act signed into law by President Barack Obama on January 29, 2009. The act amends the Civil Rights Act of 1964, stating that the 180-day statute of limitations for filing an equal-pay lawsuit regarding pay discrimination resets with each new discriminatory paycheck. It passed the House by a margin of 250 to 177, and passed the Senate 61 to 36. In all, only seven Republican members of Congress voted for the bill; the rest voted against it.[47]

A first bill to amend the statutory limitations period was introduced in the 110th United States Congress but was never enacted, as after passage by the House it failed to survive a cloture vote in the Senate due to the opposition of most Republican senators.

President Obama actively supported the Ledbetter bill. According to the official White House blog, "President Obama has long championed this bill and Lilly Ledbetter's cause, and by signing it into law, he will ensure that women like Ms. Ledbetter and other victims of pay discrimination can effectively challenge unequal pay."[48],[49]

The Family Smoking Prevention and Tobacco Control Act is a United States federal statute that was signed into law by President Barack Obama on June 22, 2009. The act gives the Food and Drug Administration the power to regulate the tobacco industry. A signature

---

[47]   "The Rachel Maddow Show," MSNBC, 4/11/2012.

[48]   "Now Comes Lilly Ledbetter." Whitehouse.gov blog. January 25, 2009.

[49]   See http://en.wikipedia.org/wiki/
Lilly_Ledbetter_Fair_Pay_Act_of_2009.

element of the law imposes new warnings and labels on tobacco packaging and its advertisements, with the goal of discouraging minors and young adults from smoking. The act also bans flavored cigarettes, places limits on the advertising of tobacco products to minors and requires tobacco companies to seek FDA approval for new tobacco products. It passed the House by a margin of 298 to 112, and passed the Senate 79 to 17.

The act:

- Creates a tobacco control center within the FDA and gives the FDA authority to regulate the content, marketing, and sale of tobacco products;
- Requires tobacco companies and importers to reveal all product ingredients and seek FDA approval for any new tobacco products;
- Allows the FDA to change tobacco product content. The ban on flavoring applies to any product meeting the definition of a "cigarette" according to Section 3(1) of the Federal Cigarette Labeling and Advertising Act. This includes any tobacco that comes rolled such as cigarettes and cigars, and added to this definition is any tobacco with the purpose to be rolled such as rolling tobacco;
- Calls for new rules to prevent sales except through direct, face-to-face exchanges between a retailer and a consumer;
- Limits advertising that could attract young smokers;
- Requires cigarette warning labels to cover 50% of the front and rear of each pack, with the word "warning" in capital letters;

- Requires FDA approval for the use of expressions such as "light," "mild," or "low" that give the impression that a particular tobacco product poses less of a health risk.

The bill makes no provisions that ban the import of the banned items for personal consumption, only for sale or distribution.

Passage of the law was supported by the American Cancer Society, whose CEO noted in a press release that the bill "forces Big Tobacco to disclose the poisons in its products and has the power to finally break the dangerous chain of addiction for generations to come."[50] The ACS press release also noted that the legislation would "require cigarette companies to disclose all ingredients used in cigarettes and to stop using words like 'light' and 'ultra-light' to give the impression that some tobacco products have a lower health risk."[51] The legislation also garnered support from the American Heart Association, whose CEO noted that the bill "provides a tremendous opportunity to finally hold tobacco companies accountable and restrict efforts to addict more children and adults."[52],[53]

The Patient Protection and Affordable Care Act (PPACA), informally referred to as Obamacare, is a United States federal statute signed into law by President Barack Obama on March 23, 2010. The law (along with the Health Care and Education Reconciliation Act of 2010) is the

---

[50]   ACS :: House Votes to Grant FDA Control of Tobacco Regulation.

[51]   Ibid.

[52]   No smoking: Historic vote could bring new limits - Yahoo! News.

[53]   See http://en.wikipedia.org/wiki/
Family_Smoking_Prevention_and_Tobacco_Control_Act.

principal health care reform legislation of the 111th United States Congress. The PPACA requires individuals not covered by employer—or government-sponsored insurance plans to maintain minimal essential health insurance coverage or pay a penalty unless exempted for religious beliefs or financial hardship, a provision commonly referred to as the "individual mandate." The act also reforms certain aspects of the private health insurance industry and public health insurance programs, increases insurance coverage of preexisting conditions, expands access to insurance to 30 million Americans, and increases projected national medical spending. Supporters claim it will slow health care cost inflation and reduce the national deficit. The CBO projects it will lower future Medicare spending.

The PPACA passed the Senate on December 24, 2009, by a vote of 60 to 39, with all Democrats and two Independents voting for and all Republicans voting against. It passed the House of Representatives on March 21, 2010, by a vote of 219 to 212, with 34 Democrats and all 178 Republicans voting against.

The PPACA includes numerous provisions to take effect over several years beginning in 2010. Policies issued before the law was promulgated are grandfathered from most federal regulations.

- A guaranteed issue and partial community rating will require insurers to offer the same premium to all applicants of the same age and geographical location without regard to most preexisting conditions (excluding tobacco use).
- A shared responsibility requirement, commonly called an "individual mandate," requires that all persons not covered by an employer-sponsored

health plan, Medicaid, Medicare, or other public insurance programs purchase and comply with an approved private insurance policy or pay a penalty, unless the applicable individual is a member of a recognized religious sect exempted by the Internal Revenue Service or waived in cases of financial hardship.

- Medicaid eligibility is expanded to include all individuals and families with incomes up to 133% of the poverty level along with a simplified CHIP (Children's Health Insurance Program) enrollment process.
- Health insurance exchanges will commence operation in each state, offering a marketplace where individuals and small businesses can compare policies and premiums and buy insurance (with a government subsidy if eligible).
- Low-income persons and families above the Medicaid level and up to 400% of the federal poverty level will receive federal subsidies on a sliding scale if they choose to purchase insurance via an exchange. (Persons at 150% of the poverty level would be subsidized such that their premium cost would be 2% of their income or $50 a month for a family of four.)
- Minimum standards for health insurance policies are to be established and annual and lifetime coverage caps will be banned.
- Firms employing 50 or more people but not offering health insurance will also pay a shared responsibility requirement if the government has had to subsidize an employee's health care.

- Very small businesses will be able to get subsidies if they purchase insurance through an exchange.
- Co-payments, co-insurance, and deductibles are to be eliminated for select health care insurance benefits considered to be part of an "essential benefits package" for Level A or Level B preventive care.
- Changes are enacted that allow a restructuring of Medicare reimbursement from "fee-for-service" to "bundled payments."
- Additional support is provided for medical research and the National Institutes of Health.

According to the Centers for Medicare and Medicaid Services, by 2019, the act will increase expenditures on Medicaid and individual subsidies by $165 billion annually while reducing Medicare expenditures by $125 billion annually. At the bill's passage into law, the CBO estimated the legislation would reduce the deficit by $143 billion over the first decade, but half of that was due to expected premiums for the C.L.A.S.S. Act, which has since been abandoned. Although the CBO generally does not provide cost estimates beyond the 10-year budget projection period (because of the great degree of uncertainty involved in the data), it decided to do so in this case at the request of lawmakers and estimated a second-decade deficit reduction of $1.2 trillion. The CBO predicted deficit reduction around a broad range of 0.5% of GDP over the 2020s while cautioning that "a wide range of changes could occur."[54]

---

[54] Farley, Robert (March 18, 2010). "Pelosi: CBO says health reform bill would cut deficits by $1.2 trillion in second decade." PolitiFact.com. Retrieved 2010-04-07.

The CBO also initially stated that the bill would "substantially reduce the growth of Medicare's payment rates for most services; impose an excise tax on insurance plans with relatively high premiums; and make various other changes to the federal tax code, Medicare, Medicaid, and other programs."[55] Under "effects on the federal deficit," in 2012, the CBO projected the act will require more than $1.7 trillion in gross federal spending over the period 2012 to 2022, some of which will be offset by penalties and tax increases related to coverage, resulting in a net increase of more than $1.2 trillion.[56]

The Dodd-Frank Wall Street Reform and Consumer Protection Act is a United States federal statute signed into law by President Barack Obama on July 21, 2010. The act implements financial regulatory reform sponsored by the Democratically controlled 111th United States Congress and the Obama administration. Passed as a response to the late-2000s recession, the act brought the most significant changes to financial regulation in the United States since the regulatory reform that followed the Great Depression, representing a significant change in the American financial regulatory environment affecting all federal financial regulatory agencies and almost every aspect of the nation's financial services industry. It passed the House by a margin of 223 to 202, and passed the Senate 59 to 39.

---

[55] "Correction Regarding the Longer-Term Effects of the Manager's Amendment to the Patient Protection and Affordable Care Act" (PDF). Congressional Budget Office. December 19, 2009. Retrieved March 22, 2010.

[56] See http://en.wikipedia.org/wiki/ Patient_Protection_and_Affordable_Care_Act.

As with other major financial reforms, some legal and financial scholars on both sides of the political spectrum have criticized the law, arguing on the one hand that the reforms were insufficient to prevent another financial crisis or additional "bailouts" of financial institutions, and on the other hand that the reforms went too far and would unduly restrict the ability of banks and other financial institutions to make loans.

In addition to the headline regulatory changes covering capital investment by banks and insurance companies, the act introduces new regulation of hedge funds and private equity funds, alters the definition of accredited investors, requires reporting by all public companies on CEO to median-employee pay ratios and other compensation data, enforces equitable access to credit for consumers, and provides incentives to promote banking among low—and medium-income residents.

The act changes the existing regulatory structure by creating a host of new agencies (while merging and removing others) in an effort to streamline the regulatory process, increasing oversight of specific institutions regarded as a systemic risk, amending the Federal Reserve Act, and promoting transparency, as well as additional changes. The act purports to provide rigorous standards and supervision to protect the economy and American consumers, investors, and businesses, purports to end taxpayer-funded bailouts of financial institutions, claims to provide for an advanced warning system on the stability of the economy, creates rules on executive compensation and corporate governance, and eliminates some of the loopholes that led to the 2008 economic recession. The new agencies are either granted explicit power over a particular aspect of financial regulation, or that power is transferred from an existing agency. All of the new agencies, and some existing ones that are not currently required to do so, are also compelled to report to Congress on an annual (or biannual) basis to present the results of current plans and to explain future goals. Important new agencies created include the Financial Stability Oversight Council, the Office of Financial Research, and the Bureau of Consumer Financial Protection.

To the extent the act impacts all federal financial regulatory agencies, eliminating one (the Office of Thrift Supervision) and creating two (the Financial Stability Oversight Council and the Office of Financial Research) in addition to several consumer protection agencies, including the Bureau of Consumer Financial Protection, this legislation in many ways represents a change in the way America's financial markets will operate in the future. Few provisions of the act became effective when the bill was signed. Only over the following 18 months, as multiple regulatory agencies write rules that implement various sections of the act, will the full importance and significance of the act be known.[57]

---

[57] See http://en.wikipedia.org/wiki/
Dodd-Frank_Wall_Street_Reform_and_Consumer_Protection_Act.

Chapter 5
Editorials

This chapter offers an overview of the relevant issues facing America in 2012. Most of them affect your daily life and the future of the country. In order to cast your vote effectively, you must familiarize yourself with these issues and each party's stance on them. Hopefully, the views expressed here will help you become more engaged in the political process.

This chapter begins with an examination of Prohibition. Organized crime flourished under the 18th Amendment, and 80 years later it remains an entrenched problem in our society. Drug trafficking, smuggling, bootlegging, counterfeiting, illegal gambling, bribery, murder, and terrorism are just some of the illegal activities crime syndicates engage in to this day.

The far right is now attempting to take similar steps on abortion rights as they did on alcohol all those years ago. (Abortion is discussed again later in this chapter.) Such measures would disproportionately disenfranchise poor and younger citizens who rely on these services. If it were up to the right, we would return once again to the days of back-alley abortions, where women would be at the mercy of amateurs and hackers and even die as a result. Poor families would be burdened with more unwanted children, thereby reducing their standards of living even further, causing poverty to escalate. Moreover, the number of unwed mothers would only increase as a consequence.[58] Social conservatives are trying to legislate their rigid view of morality on the entire population just as they did with prohibition. Prohibition did not work then and it will not work now. Will history repeat itself? Not if you exercise your vote effectively in November.

Both parties are guilty of taking their ideologies too far at different points in history. There is probably no better example of conservative overreach than the 18th Amendment. According to Wikipedia, "The proponents of prohibition had believed that banning alcoholic beverages would reduce or even eliminate many social problems, particularly drunkenness, crime, mental illness, and poverty. In fact, alcohol consumption and the incidence of alcohol-related domestic violence were *decreasing* before the 18th Amendment was adopted. Following the imposition of prohibition, reformers 'were dismayed to find that child neglect and violence against children actually increased during the Prohibition era.'

"During Prohibition, people continued to produce and drink alcohol, and bootlegging helped foster a massive industry completely under the control of organized crime. Drinking in speakeasies became increasingly fashionable, and many mothers worried about the allure that alcohol and other illegal activities associated with bootlegging would have over their children.

"Prohibitionists argued that prohibition would be more effective if enforcement were increased. However,

---

[58]   See http://www.pro-truth.net/49-if-abortion-was-illegal.html.

increased efforts to enforce prohibition simply resulted in the government spending *more* money, rather than less. The economic cost of prohibition became especially pronounced during the Great Depression. According to the Association Against the Prohibition Amendment (AAPA) and Women's Organization for National Prohibition Reform (WONPR), an estimated $861 million was lost in federal tax revenue from untaxed liquor, while $40 million was spent annually on prohibition enforcement. The AAPA has also released a pamphlet claiming that $11 billion was lost in federal liquor-tax revenue and that $310 million was spent on prohibition enforcement from 1920 to 1931. This lack of potential funding during a period of economic strife became a crucial part of the campaign for repeal.

"During this period, support for prohibition diminished among voters and politicians. John D. Rockefeller, Jr., a lifelong nondrinker who had contributed much money to the Prohibitionist Anti-Saloon League, eventually announced his support for repeal because of the widespread problems he believed prohibition had caused. The repeal movement also attracted a substantial portion of women, defying the assumption that recently enfranchised female voters would automatically vote as a bloc on the issue. They became pivotal in the effort to repeal, as many came to the painful conclusion that the destructiveness of alcohol was now embodied in Prohibition itself."[59] The main accomplishment of Prohibition was the creation of an elaborate organized American crime network. Ultimately, the most effective way to combat alcohol abuse is through comprehensive public education programs much like those applied to tobacco products.

---

[59]   See http://en.wikipedia.org/wiki/Repeal_of_Prohibition.

The 2012 Republican presidential primaries are complete and former Massachusetts Governor Mitt Romney has since become the Republican nominee largely due to oppressive negative ads waged against his opponents, a pattern his campaign has continued against President Obama in the general election. Rather than dive into the muck and mire of campaign politics, this book will refrain from discussing Romney's stance on various topics. Instead, it will address enduring issues at the heart of *both* campaigns. It would be safe to summarize Romney's platform by saying he takes the opposite view of the president in most cases.

I will close out this topic with commentary by former New York Governor Eliot Spitzer, beginning with a quote from Mitt Romney:

> "Either the individual pays, or the taxpayers pay. A free ride on government is not libertarian . . . An uninsured libertarian might counter that he could refuse the free payer, but under the law that is impossible and inhumane." Thus spoke Romney 1.0, pre-Etch-a-Sketch, pre-desperate to appease the far-right fringe of an already far-right party. And of course, Romney 1.0 was correct: for universal coverage to work, the individual mandate is essential. That is exactly why President Obama, then Sen. Hillary Rodham Clinton, the Congress, Newt Gingrich, the Heritage Foundation—all agreed with then Gov. Mitt Romney's logic and supported the individual mandate. Romney now tries to pretend that this irrefutable logic might apply to a state, but not to the federal government.

That is pure rubbish. But there is something more fundamental, something that goes beyond merely flip-flopping on one issue. There is a central lack of a core integrity to Mitt Romney. He has flopped on every issue of significance—moving at each moment wherever the political wind might take him. This lack of constancy on every social, economic, foreign policy issue should be an immediate disqualifier for somebody who wants to be president. Above all, that job requires the fortitude to stand up and make—and then explain—unpopular decisions. The willingness to educate the public when a tough decision is required. But think about this: Mitt was Keynesian before he wasn't. He was pro-choice before he was anti-choice. He was pro-same-sex marriage before he was not. He was for the individual mandate before he was against it. When somebody has no core, he can't be trusted. And when somebody can't be trusted, he should not be president.[60]

Health care is a necessity, but who will pay for it? If you happen to be covered, your health insurance contributes. If you are *not* covered, the health care provider pays for it out of pocket. Is this reasonable and appropriate? Why should a hospital pay for an uninsured patient treated in an emergency room, thereby raising insurance premiums for the covered? The logical conclusion is to have everyone covered by some form of health insurance. This is the justification for the individual mandate of the Affordable Care Act,

---

[60] "Viewpoint with Eliot Spitzer," CURRENT, 6/6/2012.

also known as Obamacare. The mandate constitutes a tax under Congress' authority to raise and collect taxes on those without health insurance. The conservative argument is that while everyone needs food, the government has no right to make you buy broccoli. But there is a big difference between food and health care: If you don't buy broccoli, someone else doesn't have to pay for you to eat[61] (unless, of course, you go to a soup kitchen, and even then the costs involved are more manageable in comparison). Food prices are also affordable for most—not so with health care, the costs of which can be astronomical. An effective, stable health insurance market requires everyone's participation.

Republicans have vehemently opposed the Affordable Care Act from its inception. In spite of all its helpful provisions, they would rather cater to their constituents: health insurance companies. This was evidenced on July 11, 2012, when House Republicans voted to repeal Obamacare for the 33rd time. For commentary on this action, I turn to former Governor Eliot Spitzer:

> On Wednesday, the House of Representatives voted to reverse President Obama's Affordable Care Act for the 33rd time. The 32 other times all got shot down by the Democratically-controlled Senate and that's exactly what is going to happen this time, too. The vote was a giant waste of time and everyone knew that before they started. But time isn't the only thing Republicans wasted here, which brings us to our number of the day: $48 million. That's how much the pointless votes have cost the American

---

61   "Hardball with Chris Matthews," MSNBC, 3/26/2012 & 3/27/2012.

taxpayer. The party that keeps yelling for spending cuts is once again squandering money. These vain attempts at repeal add up to at least 80 hours of time on the House floor which . . . have cost $48 million. All this just so Republicans can posture once more, beating the dead horse of their opposition to health care reform. Meanwhile, the GOP expended no time or money proposing an alternative health plan or voting on the President's jobs bill or coming up with their own jobs bill. No, this was just $48 million for political posing—everyone knows it, and you paid for it. Maybe we could bill this to the Republican National Committee. [62]

Considering the ACA was modeled after Romneycare in Massachusetts, Republicans need to seriously question their opposition to the plan.

The debate over birth control in this country rages on. As of 2012, eight states already mandate that employers provide contraception coverage in their health insurance policies, even if the employer is a religious institution. In an effort to respect the religious consciences of such institutions, President Obama modified health care reform at the national level to exempt them from having to pay for contraceptive insurance by requiring that insurance companies do so instead. This provision is less intrusive than that in the eight states mentioned above, yet conservatives still oppose it. This is nothing short of hypocrisy, since in 2006 then Governor Mitt Romney signed a health care overhaul in Massachusetts requiring a contraceptive

---

[62] "Viewpoint with Eliot Spitzer," CURRENT, 7/12/2012.

mandate, as did Mike Huckabee in Arkansas and other Republican governors. If such a mandate was good for Republicans then, it should be good for them now.

Despite claims to the contrary, the Blunt-Rubio amendment would have enabled employers to deny *any* health coverage to their female employees on religious or moral grounds. This is a serious, inexcusable breach of women's fundamental health care rights. Even Republican Senator Lisa Murkowski voiced her dissatisfaction: "I regretted the vote on the Blunt Amendment; it was in direct reflection to . . . women feeling that the party I have chosen to affiliate myself with, the Republican Party, is ignoring their concerns, is causing them to feel like the rights they believed were settled a long time ago are now being threatened, possibly eroded . . . It makes no sense to attack women, and if you don't view this as an attack on women, then you need to go home, you need to talk to your wives, you need to go talk to your daughters. Ask them if they feel that this is an attack, because this is how women are perceiving the situation."[63] Contraceptive rights have been an accepted part of our society for 50 years. Why is it suddenly an issue on the right?

Most reasonable people would prefer not to see abortions happen. Nevertheless, unwanted pregnancies are a reality, and sometimes it is in the best interest of the mother to have them terminated, with more notable cases being rape and incest. Though abortion is legal under the Constitution, many conservative governors and state legislatures have passed legislation restricting it. In April 2012, Wisconsin

---

[63]   "The Rachel Maddow Show," MSNBC, 4/6/2012.

passed a law that blocks insurance coverage for all abortions. They also passed a law removing contraception from sex education curriculums, instead requiring teachers to stress abstinence as the only sure way to prevent pregnancy and STDs.[64]

Such legislatures have also made it a requirement that women undergo an ultrasound before receiving an abortion. These ultrasounds are completely medically unnecessary. They are imposed regardless of the advice of the woman's physician, and the financial burden for them is placed upon the taxpayer. To mandate a medically unnecessary procedure *and* demand the woman pay for it out of pocket is nothing short of an outrage. Such measures are part of an effort to inhibit abortions from taking place, but the most sensible method for discouraging abortions remains the promotion of contraception use.[65] It is better to deal with the circumstance *before* it happens rather than after.

Electoral or voter fraud is defined as "illegal interference with the process of an election."[66] WashingtonPost.com reports that, in fact, "Prosecutable cases of voter fraud are rare. For example, a 2005 statewide study in Ohio found four instances of ineligible persons voting or attempting to vote in 2002 and 2004, out of 9 million votes cast. An investigation of fraud allegations in Wisconsin in 2004 led to the prosecution of 0.0007 percent of voters." In particular, state photo ID restrictions "disproportionately affect African Americans, Latinos, young voters, people

---

64   Ibid.

65   "Hardball with Chris Matthews," MSNBC, 5/17/2012.

66   See http://en.wikipedia.org/wiki/Voter_fraud.

over 65 and people with disabilities. Advancement Project studies show that 11 percent of eligible voters, or about 21 million people, don't have updated, state-issued photo IDs," namely:

- 25 percent of African Americans,
- 15 percent of those earning less than $35,000,
- 18 percent of citizens age 65 or older, and
- 20 percent of voters age 18 to 29.[67]

This means that the only real goal accomplished by state photo ID requirements is the disenfranchisement of such groups. Practices like these were supposedly outlawed by the Civil Rights Acts of 1957 and 1960. Proponents of the new regulations claim that because photo ID is required to purchase items such as alcohol and airplane tickets and to cash checks, it should be required to vote as well. The difference is that liquor, plane tickets, and checks are all *privileges*, while voting is a *right* guaranteed by the Constitution.

As Wikipedia explains, "In some cases voters may be invalidly disenfranchised, which is true electoral fraud. For example . . . corrupt election officials may misuse voting regulations such as a literacy test or requirement for proof of identity or address in such a way as to make it difficult or impossible for their targets to cast a vote. If such practices discriminate against a religious or ethnic group, they may so distort the political process that the political order becomes grossly unrepresentative, as in the post-Reconstruction or Jim Crow era until the Voting Rights Act of 1965."[68]

---

[67] See http://www.washingtonpost.com/opinions/five-myths-about-voter-fraud/2011/10/04/ gIQAkjoYTL_story.html.

[68] See http://en.wikipedia.org/wiki/Voter_fraud.

Washingtonpost.com further states that "[t]he push for photo ID laws and other restrictions is largely championed by the GOP and conservative groups. Record rates of voter registration and turnout among young and minority voters in 2008 affected federal races across the nation, as about two-thirds of new voters registered as Democrats in the 29 states that record party affiliation. The 2010 midterms put more conservatives in office who want to combat this trend. The right-wing American Legislative Exchange Council, for example, drafted and promoted photo ID legislation that was introduced in more than 30 states."[69] One hundred fifty voter suppression laws have been introduced in these various state legislatures. Because of such efforts, five million eligible Americans will find it harder to exercise their right to vote in November. The most common suppression tactics include government-issued photo ID requirements, the restriction of registration drives, limitations on early voting, and the imposition of onerous residency requirements. Since minorities, the poor, and the young typically vote Democratic, it is clear that conservative state legislatures imposing these restrictions are attempting nothing short of the suppression of such demographic group votes. In effect, Republicans are using every tactic they can to stop our democracy from actually selecting the candidate with the most support, particularly when that candidate is a Democrat.[70] In other words, Republicans would rather "steal" an election than win it fairly.

There is no better evidence of such efforts than the statement made by Republican State Rep. Mike Turzai

---

[69] See http://www.washingtonpost.com/opinions/five-myths-about-voter-fraud/2011/10/04/ gIQAkjoYTL_story.html.

[70] "The War Room with Jennifer Granholm," CURRENT, 5/22/2012.

of Pennsylvania during a speech in which he listed accomplishments made by the legislature during the current session: "Voter ID, which is going to allow Governor Romney to win the state of Pennsylvania—done!"[71]

Another example of Republican overreach is the stripping of collective bargaining rights in Wisconsin. In 2011, a series of protests were waged in the state beginning in February that at their heights involved as many as 100,000 protestors opposing the Wisconsin Budget Repair Bill. The bill consisted of legislation proposed by Republican Governor Scott Walker and passed by the Wisconsin Legislature to address a projected $3.6 billion budget deficit; included within the bill was a provision to limit collective bargaining for most public employees.[72] Subsequently, anti-tax activists and other conservatives, including Tea Party advocates, launched small pockets of counter protests. In July of that year, workers from two local chapters of the AFL-CIO filed a lawsuit against the law, alleging it violated the U.S. Constitution's equal protection clause by limiting collective bargaining only for public workers. While public unions have the right to collectively bargain in about 30 states, Virginia and Texas prohibit formal collective bargaining with public employees and many other states are considering making changes to their collective bargaining policies.[73]

The real purpose of the bill was not to remedy a budget shortfall, but to eliminate unions from the state altogether.

---

[71] "Politics Nation," MSNBC, 8/15/2012.

[72] See http://en.wikipedia.org/wiki/Wisconsin_Budget_Repair_Bill.

[73] See http://en.wikipedia.org/wiki/2011_Wisconsin_protests.

To demonstrate this point, in the 2010 election cycle, six of the top 10 campaign contributors supported Republican candidates and comprised corporations. Only three of the top 10 contributors supported Democrats and comprised unions. While individual donations are helpful, big money in politics comes either from corporations, which disproportionately support Republicans, or unions, which disproportionately support Democrats. Although corporate support is varied, large-funded Democratic support comes from one source: unions.[74]

Eliminating unions means eliminating the Democrats' ability to compete in elections on a large scale. Even though union membership has declined steadily over the past 60 years, it is still going strong in the public sector. The motivation behind Governor Walker's union-busting bill is not a budget crisis. Neither is it more jobs, because Walker has racked up the single worst jobs record in the country since eradicating public union rights in the state. When asked by a wealthy campaign donor whether Wisconsin will ever embrace "right to work" and become a "red state," Walker gave a response off the record that revealed his hidden agenda: "Well, we're going to start in a couple of weeks with our budget adjustment bill. The first step is we're going to deal with collective bargaining for all public employee unions, because you use divide and conquer."[75]

The public protests were a major driving force behind the recall election that saw two incumbent Republican state senators defeated by Democratic challengers in 2011 and an effort to recall Governor Walker along with four other

---

[74]   "The Rachel Maddow Show," MSNBC, 5/24/2012.

[75]   Ibid.

Republican state senators. On January 17, 2012, United Wisconsin, the coalition that spearheaded the recall effort along with the Democratic Party, said that one million signatures were collected, far exceeding the 540,208 needed to recall, amounting to 23% of the state's eligible voters, just shy of the 1.1 million votes earned by Walker. On March 30, 2012, the Government Accountability Board unanimously ruled in favor of the recall. The recall election for both Governor Walker and Lieutenant Governor Kleefisch was allowed to take place on Tuesday, June 5, 2012.[76]

Walker and Kleefisch wound up winning that recall by a seven-point margin in the first test of a post-Citizens United election. The proof of the decision's effect is in the numbers: Walker raised a total of $30.5 million, 66% of which came from outside the state. On the other hand, his opponent Tom Barrett raised only $3.9 million, 26% of which came from out of state.[77] It is clear Walker's 7.5-to-1 spending advantage played a big role in his victory.[78] David Shuster, correspondent for *Current TV*, contends that Democrats spent too much time and money during the primary promoting their candidate instead of combating Walker's negative campaign ads, which were airing at that time. When the primary concluded and the Democrats had their nominee, they only had a few weeks to publicize Walker's negativity before the recall election, a period of time that proved to be too short to successfully campaign against all of his prior advertising.[79] All was not lost, however, as Democrats regained control of the state Senate by winning

---

[76] See http://en.wikipedia.org/wiki/Scott_Walker_(politician).

[77] "The Rachel Maddow Show," MSNBC, 6/5/2012.

[78] "The Ed Show," MSNBC, 6/6/2012.

[79] "Viewpoint with Eliot Spitzer," CURRENT, 6/5/2012.

one of the four recalled Senate contests mentioned above. In the end, it came down to turnout: The Democrats were not successful in getting out the vote. Those who failed to vote will have to live with their decision and Walker's radical agenda until he comes up for reelection in 2014.

In spite of the popular right-wing complaint over a supposed lack of adequate American oil production under President Obama, oil production has increased in the past three years, to the point where the U.S. now exports more oil than it imports. In contrast, production consistently decreased during President Bush's two terms. We are now producing more oil than we have in the last eight years. On top of that, demand is at its lowest level since 1997, indicating the problem is not one of supply and demand. The right's perennial solution to high gas prices is the mantra "drill, baby drill." Apparently, being a net exporter of oil is not good enough. The right is unwilling to address speculation on Wall Street, which is the real cause of high energy prices. The purpose of speculation is simple: to drive up the price of oil as high as it will go in order to make profit, regardless of the consequences to the general public. Over 80% of the oil futures market is controlled not by entities that actually use oil, but by Wall Street speculators.[80] A March 2012 St. Louis Federal Reserve Bank study found that after global demand, speculation was the second largest contributor to oil prices and accounted for about 15% of the rise in price. Michael Greenberger, former director of trading and markets for the Commodity Futures Trading Commission, has stated that removing excessive speculation

---

[80]   "The Ed Show," MSNBC, 3/21/2012.

from the market would result in "a dramatic surprise to the American people how low the price of gasoline would go."[81] The Dodd-Frank bill is designed to limit such speculation, yet Republicans in Congress are striving to repeal it, accusing it of being too much regulation. Such regulation is the only thing Wall Street speculators understand.

———————

Most reasonable people would agree that wars should be fought only as a last resort. Such was not the case with the 2003 Iraq War. The principle premise for the 2003 Iraq War, as stated in the Iraq War Resolution of 2002, was the Bush administration's claims that Saddam Hussein possessed weapons of mass destruction, that such weapons were an imminent threat to the United States, and that al-Qaeda was operating within Iraq. All three claims proved to be false. These claims were built on faulty intelligence and resulted in eight years of war, nearly 4,500 dead, and over 32,000 wounded. The war was supposed to be over in a matter of weeks. Iraqi oil was supposed to help pay for it, and each Iraqi citizen was supposed to welcome America with open arms. None of these scenarios actually happened. Rather than granting weapons inspectors enough time to determine the presence of WMDs, the neocons rushed the war resolution through Congress, ultimately using the toppling of Saddam Hussein and the opportunity to engage in democratic nation building as justification.

———————

Until 2005, the American right of self-defense involving firearms was typically decided by a court of law. The case of

---

81   "CBS Evening News with Scott Pelley," CBS, 4/17/2012.

James Workman, a 77-year-old Pensacola man who fatally shot an intruder who entered the trailer Workman and his wife were living in after hurricane Ivan damaged their home in 2004, resulted in a push from Florida lawmakers to pass sweeping self-defense legislation that would become known as the "stand your ground" law.

Many criminal law doctrines evolve over centuries, but "stand your ground" laws arrived very suddenly. Under traditional legal principles, people in disputes generally have a duty to "deescalate" the situation in the interest of saving human lives. The Florida law lowered the bar on the historic "duty to retreat." Now, people have the same kind of right to stand their ground in public—on streets, in parking lots and bars—that they have had historically in their homes.

After gaining a foothold in Florida, where the law passed 39 to 0 in the state Senate and 94 to 20 in the state House, the "stand your ground" movement expanded quickly to more than two dozen other states.[82] This legal revolution did not just happen. The National Rifle Association (NRA) and its allies (such as the American Legislative Exchange Council, or ALEC) lobbied for the changes heavily, arguing for "stand your ground" as an important gun right. The lobbying effort paid off. As of today, 25 states have passed similar laws.

Critics have pointed out the obvious problem with "stand your ground" laws. They encourage people who get caught up in dangerous encounters to up the ante and shoot when

---

[82] See http://www.tampabay.com/blogs/the-buzz-florida-politics/content/floridas-stand-your-ground-law-was-born-2004-case-story-has-been-distorted.

gunfire could be avoided. The Brady Campaign to Prevent Gun Violence, a gun control advocacy group, has dubbed "stand your ground" laws as "shoot first" laws. Further, the National District Attorneys Association (NDAA) has pointed out an oddity of "stand your ground:" the "blanket immunity" that the Florida law gives to members of the public who fire their guns is actually broader than the leeway the law gives to police officers themselves, whose job it is to defend public safety.

There is evidence that these laws encourage people to turn tense encounters into killings. As Ideas.time.com reports, "Five years after Florida's 'stand your ground' law took effect, the *Tampa Bay Times* found that justifiable homicides in Florida had 'spiked': up from an average of 34 in the first half of the past decade to 105 in 2009. The *Washington Post* has reported that other states have seen similar jumps. It is not just people who are parties to these encounters who have to worry. As the NDAA has pointed out, needless use of firearms in public places also puts innocent bystanders at risk. The 'stand your ground' principle encourages people in uncertain situations to shoot first and ask questions later, and makes it far more likely that such situations will result in fatalities."[83] These laws must adopt significant reform or repeal before any more questionable deaths occur.

The Great Recession was the worst economic crisis since the Great Depression. Evaluating the best methods for resolving it requires a look back at the policies that

---

[83]   See http://ideas.time.com/2012/04/16/the-growing-movement-to-repeal-stand-your-ground-laws/.

helped cause it. In their lengthy 2008 investigative article for the *Washington Post* titled "What Went Wrong," authors Anthony Faiola, Ellen Nakashima, and Jill Drew claim that former Federal Reserve Board Chairman Alan Greenspan, Treasury Secretary Robert Rubin, and SEC Chairman Arthur Levitt vehemently opposed any regulation of financial instruments known as derivatives. They further claim that Greenspan actively sought to undermine the office of the Commodity Futures Trading Commission when the office tried to initiate regulation of derivatives. Ultimately, it was the collapse of a specific kind of derivative, the mortgage-backed security, that triggered the economic crisis of 2008.[84] In short, according to Phil Angelides, former chairman of the Financial Crisis Inquiry Commission, the crisis was brought on by "egregious predatory lending, mortgage fraud rampant across the country, regulators asleep at the wheel, [and] unbridled, unconstrained recklessness by Wall Street firms and their CEOs driven by compensation that rewarded them for making the big deal without regard to the long-term consequences."[85]

President George W. Bush signed the Troubled Asset Relief Program (TARP) into law in 2008 to initially deal with the problem. The TARP was a government program designed to purchase assets and equity from financial institutions to strengthen the financial sector. It was a component of the government's measures to address the subprime mortgage crisis. The TARP originally authorized expenditures of $700 billion and was expected to cost U.S. taxpayers as much as $300 billion. By March 2012, the

---

[84]   See http://en.wikipedia.org/wiki/Great_recession.

[85]   "Viewpoint with Eliot Spitzer," CURRENT, 5/31/2012.

CBO stated that disbursements would total $431 billion and estimated the total cost at $32 billion.[86]

Since the TARP was not sufficient to solve all of the country's financial woes, President Obama signed the American Recovery and Reinvestment Act (ARRA) into law in 2009. The primary objective for ARRA was to save and create jobs almost immediately. The approximate cost of the economic stimulus package was estimated to be $787 billion at the time of passage. The act included direct spending on infrastructure, education, health, energy, federal tax incentives, and expansion of unemployment benefits and other social welfare provisions.[87]

To institute financial regulatory reform so that such a crisis would hopefully not happen again, the Dodd-Frank Wall Street Reform and Consumer Protection Act was signed into law in 2010. It brought the most significant changes to financial regulation in the United States since the regulatory reform following the Great Depression. These actions represented a significant change in the American financial regulatory environment, affecting all federal financial regulatory agencies and almost every aspect of the nation's financial services industry.

Despite these interventions, the economic rebound continues to lag behind. Additional measures to stimulate the economy have consistently been thwarted by Republicans in Congress. For example, the American Jobs Act (AJA) proposed by President Obama in 2011 represented a major new jobs package that would not have added to the national

---

[86]   See http://en.wikipedia.org/wiki/Troubled_Asset_Relief_Program.

[87]   See http://en.wikipedia.org/wiki/ARRA.

deficit and would have been fully paid for. It included such measures as:

- Cutting and suspending $245 billion worth of payroll taxes for qualifying employers and 160 million medium—to low-income employees;
- Both new and preexisting desperately needed infrastructure projects;
- Additional funding to protect the jobs of teachers, police officers, and firefighters;
- Modernizing at least 35,000 public schools and community colleges;
- Hiring construction workers to help rehabilitate and refurbish hundreds of thousands of foreclosed homes and businesses;
- Creating additional regulations on businesses who discriminate against hiring those who are long-term unemployed; and
- Loosening regulations on small businesses that wish to raise capital, while retaining investor protections.[88]

Despite the bill receiving a 63% approval rating from the public,[89] it failed to garner the necessary 60 votes in the Senate to proceed and hence was defeated by a lack of support from Republicans, who never gave it a chance to work. Independent economists estimate that the policies set forth in the AJA could have added as many as two million jobs to the economy and boosted GDP growth by as much as 2%. It was also defeated because it would have benefitted the president's reelection chances in November. As

---

[88]   See http://en.wikipedia.org/wiki/American_jobs_act.

[89]   "The Rachel Maddow Show," MSNBC, 4/16/2012.

Republican Senator Mitch McConnell's stated number one goal reflects, "the single most important thing [Republicans want] to achieve is for President Obama to be a one-term president."[90]

Despite such setbacks, bright spots remain in the economy. Chrysler's profits for the first quarter of 2012 were its best in 13 years—more than quadruple the same period in 2011.[91] General Motors is once again the biggest auto manufacturer in the world, and since March 2010, the country has achieved 31 straight months of private sector job growth. This progress should continue if President Obama is reelected, Democrats retain control of the Senate, and obstructionist Republicans lose control of the House in November.

———————

In spite of the well-known causes of the Great Recession, banks have not yet learned their lessons. On May 10, 2012, "too big to fail" firm JPMorgan Chase stunned investors by announcing a $2 billion trading loss resulting from investment in risky derivatives, which were at the heart of the financial crisis in 2008. According to the *New York Times*, that loss rose to upwards of $9 billion by June 28. Further, according to Huffingtonpost.com, "more than three years after the financial industry almost collapsed, the colossal misfire was cited as proof that big banks still do not understand the threats posed by their own speculation . . . JPMorgan is the largest bank in the United States and was the only major bank to remain profitable during the 2008

———————

90   "The War Room with Jennifer Granholm," CURRENT, 6/1/2012.

91   See http://detroit.cbslocal.com/2012/04/26/chrysler-quadruples-quarterly-profit/.

financial crisis. That lent credibility to its tough-talking CEO, Jamie Dimon, as he opposed stricter regulation in the aftermath."[92] In response, JPMorgan has spent more than $21 million dollars over the past three years on lobbying for looser regulations, the most of any bank.[93]

Dimon responded to the trading losses: "In hindsight, the new strategy was flawed, complex, poorly reviewed, poorly executed and poorly monitored. It's obvious at this point that . . . there were many errors, sloppiness and bad judgement."[94] As the Huffington Post explains, "JPMorgan's disclosure recharged a debate about how to ensure that banks are strong and competitive without allowing them to become so big and complex that they threaten the financial system when they falter. The JPMorgan loss did not cause anything close to the panic that followed the September 2008 failure of the Lehman Brothers investment bank. But it shook the confidence of the financial industry . . . Enhanced oversight of derivatives was a pillar of the 2010 financial overhaul law, known as Dodd-Frank, but the implementation has been delayed repeatedly and will not take effect until the end of this year at the earliest. JPMorgan's trades show that the derivatives market remains too opaque for regulators to oversee effectively, said Rep. Barney Frank, D-Mass., one of the law's namesakes."[95]

---

[92]   http://www.huffingtonpost.com/2012/05/12/jpmorgan-chase-trading-loss-loss-regulation_n_1511595.html.

[93]   "CBS Evening News with Scott Pelley," CBS, 5/14/2012.

[94]   "Viewpoint with Eliot Spitzer," CURRENT, 5/11/2012.

[95]   See http://www.huffingtonpost.com/2012/05/12/jpmorgan-chase-trading-loss-loss-regulation_n_1511595.html.

Huffingtonpost.com further observes that "immediately after the [2008] crisis, a time of popular outrage over bailouts and investment losses, there was broad public support for an overhaul of bank regulations. The changes promoted by the Obama administration were in many cases similar to what the financial industry had sought before the crisis: consolidation of regulators and oversight of the multi-trillion-dollar marketplace for derivatives. Regulators are still drafting hundreds of rules under the 2010 law. As Wall Street has returned to record profits, and executives to million-dollar bonuses, banks have fought to soften those rules. In particular, the industry has fought hard against a few provisions that might have prevented the problems at JPMorgan. One is the so-called Volcker rule, which will prohibit banks from trading for their own profit. The rule is still being written, and the Federal Reserve has said it will begin enforcement in 2014."[96]

Dimon sits on the board of the New York Fed, the organization responsible for overseeing and regulating his bank—and the group he thinks should relax the rules for his type of risky trading. To alleviate any conflict of interest, Dimon should resign from the Fed board, acknowledge that he cannot be on the board while simultaneously lobbying it, and admit that he does not control the risk in his own organization. For a decade, the Fed has failed to pick up on significant Wall Street threats such as excess leverage, sub-prime fraud, and dangerous concentrations of risk in companies that are "too big to fail," largely because the Fed contains the very voices that helped cause the failure in the first place.[97]

---

[96]   Ibid.

[97]   "Viewpoint with Eliot Spitzer," CURRENT, 5/14/2012.

Consequences have already begun to be realized at Chase. On May 14, the bank replaced Ina Drew, chief investment officer and one of the highest-ranking women on Wall Street, with Matthew E. Zames and appointed a former chief financial officer, Mike Cavanagh, to head up the task of fixing what went wrong. Mr. Cavanagh is one of the most respected senior executives at the bank. He has been a loyal lieutenant of Mr. Dimon' since before Dimon took over JPMorgan Chase and has been discussed as a possible successor.[98] Such responses are not enough; so long as greed is the driving force behind Wall Street, strict regulations are necessary to keep firms like Chase from creating financial disasters like the Great Recession from happening again.

It is interesting to note that over the last 50 years, private sector jobs have increased much more under Democratic administrations than Republican ones. In particular, 42 million jobs were added in 23 years of Democratic presidents, while only 24 million were added in 28 years of Republican rule. Stocks invested under Democratic control of the White House produced nine times the return than during Republican control. The United States posted a budget surplus of $60 billion in April 2012. The Wall Street Journal and the Financial Times have reported that over $500 billion dollars in state budget gaps have been closed across the nation.[99]

---

[98] See http://dealbook.nytimes.com/2012/05/14/warnings-said-to-go-unheeded-by-chase-bosses/.

[99] "The War Room with Jennifer Granholm," CURRENT, 5/10/2012.

Republicans consistently advocate tax cuts to stimulate the economy, claiming Democratic plans to tax the wealthiest 1% in America amount to "class warfare." Their explanation for their insistence on *cutting* taxes for the wealthiest 1% is the failed Reagan policy of trickle-down (or top-down) economics. George W. Bush and the Republican Congress passed unfunded tax cuts in 2001 and 2003 and the result was a rise of only three million jobs over eight years,[100] along with a dramatic increase in the federal deficit. During that time, the rich only got richer and poverty increased in turn. Contrast that with a rise of four million jobs over the first three years of the Obama administration.[101] What the country needs is "bottom-up economics:" if employees are paid higher salaries and their benefits are enhanced, they will become more productive, thereby making their respective companies more profitable and competitive in turn. The more profitable and competitive their companies are, the better the effect on our overall economy.[102]

In the past 30 years,

- income for the wealthiest 1% has increased by a staggering 275%,
- while income for the middle 60% has grown by just 40%, and
- the lowest 20% has only grown by 18%.[103]

---

[100]   "The Ed Show," MSNBC, 4/6/2012.

[101]   Ibid.

[102]   See http://archive.blisstree.com/live/top-down-v-bottom-up-economics-101-28/.

[103]   http://en.wikipedia.org/wiki/Income_inequality_in_the_United_States.

The income inequality represented by these statistics truly amounts to class warfare. We cannot exacerbate this problem by giving more tax breaks to the rich when we already have the most unequal distribution of wealth and income of any major nation on Earth, far greater than at any time since the 1920s. For example, 93% of all new income created in 2010 went to the top 1%. That means the whole economy (all economic growth) has made the richest people richer, steadily increasing worker productivity and forcing ordinary people to work longer hours for lower wages as a result.[104] Furthermore, median family net worth fell from $126,400 in 2007 to $77,300 in 2010, a drop of almost 39% and the lowest number since 1992, according to the Federal Reserve.[105] Surely, the middle class requires some form of economic relief.

If anyone's taxes need to be cut, it is the lower 99%, not the wealthy. Congress needs to pass the "Buffett Rule," which calls for raising taxes to a minimum rate of 30% on individuals earning more than $1 million a year. It is only fair that the wealthy pay the same rate as the middle class. In March 2012, the non-partisan United States Congress Joint Committee on Taxation released a letter estimating that the Buffett Rule would raise "$4.67 billion per year over the next 10 years."[106] In an April 2012 CNN/ORC International poll, 72% of all Americans favored the rule.[107] While this kind of measure is long overdue and would begin to address income inequality in America, it will have to wait for a Democratic-controlled Congress to pass. Republicans

---

[104] "The Ed Show," MSNBC, 5/25/2012.

[105] "Viewpoint with Eliot Spitzer," CURRENT, 6/11/2012.

[106] See http://en.wikipedia.org/wiki/Buffett_Rule.

[107] "The Ed Show," MSNBC, 4/16/2012.

defeated such a bill in the Senate in the same month the poll was taken.[108] This defeat emphasizes that Republicans need to seriously confront inequality issues before making economic policies.

The president has since proposed to extend the Bush-era tax cuts for the 98% of Americans earning less than $250,000 per year, and allow the tax cuts to expire for those making more, excluding the first $250,000. As indicated previously, there is no evidence that lowering taxes on the wealthy increases jobs. On the contrary, the economy created 23 million new jobs and the biggest budget surplus in history under President Clinton, the decade *before* the Bush tax cuts were implemented when the top rate was 39.6%. The country stands behind this fact: In an April 2012 Gallop poll, 62% of Americans said rich people pay too little in taxes; only 25% said they pay their fair share. The fact is the most effective way to raise jobs is to lower taxes on the middle class.[109] Lowering taxes on the middle class creates disposable income, which in turn stimulates the economy. And stimulating the economy is supposed to create jobs, not make rich people richer while making poor people poorer.

I will conclude this topic with commentary on tax policy from former Governor Eliot Spitzer:

> The entirety of Mitt Romney's economic agenda—and the agenda of the Republican Party (led by Grover Norquist) for the past quarter of a century—has been to cut marginal tax rates for

---

[108] See http://www.rawstory.com/rs/2012/04/16/senate-republicans-block-buffett-rule-bill/.

[109] "The Ed Show," MSNBC, 7/9/2012.

the wealthy. The elixir to stimulate growth, as they have repeated so often that it has become a mantra, is to give so-called job-creators the incentive to invest by cutting their marginal rates. We have seen the historical failure of this argument here at home. Gross Domestic Product and job growth were much greater than they are now when marginal tax rates were higher, whether you look at the 1990s or back to World War II, when marginal rates were at about 90 percent, compared with 35 percent now. But let's look at the argument from another perspective: Let's compare GDP growth and unemployment here at home with those rates in other countries where the marginal tax rate is much higher. Take Sweden, for instance, which has a marginal tax rate of 57 percent. Japan's is 50 percent and Germany's is 45 percent—all significantly higher than the 35 percent rate here. Since 2004, the GDP growth rates for those countries have been comparable to ours, often exceeding it. And when it comes to unemployment, we have had a consistently higher unemployment rate than they have since the cataclysm of 2008. So what should we conclude from this? One of my favorite sayings in life is: Challenge the premise. The entire premise of the Republican worldview is that we must cut marginal tax rates, even if it means starving critical investments and letting the social safety next get frayed. Their argument—in its entirety—about the virtue and necessity of lower tax rates is wrong. When we look at the past 50 years of U.S. history and the record of growth in other industrialized nations, the data prove that the Republicans' claim of a causal link between low marginal tax rates and economic vitality is flawed. This false premise is the heart and soul of Gov. Romney's [and the Republican Party's] economic agenda. Challenge [their] premise—it is wrong.[110]

Since at least January, Republican Speaker of the House John Boehner has been complaining about 30 jobs bills that have passed the House but remain stalled in the Senate. His assertion is as follows: "These aren't big controversial bills that no one has read. They're practical, common sense proposals to help small businesses to create jobs and build a stronger economy for all Americans. We're going to keep adding to this pile and we're going to keep calling on President Obama and Democrats in the Senate to give these jobs bills a vote."[111] A closer look at these bills reveals their true nature: Nine of them deal with stripping away the EPA's ability to protect public health, eight diminish the government's broader regulatory power, three aim to open up waters for more off-shore drilling, two alter rules for the formation of unions (not surprisingly making it more difficult if not impossible to do so), one is a resolution pushing for the Keystone XL pipeline, one is a proposal to open up the Tonto National Forest for copper mining, and another is a resolution disapproving Internet neutrality. Only one bill actually deals directly with creating job opportunities: H.R. 3012—the Fairness for High School Immigrants Act of 2011, which makes it easier for companies to hire highly

---

110   "Viewpoint with Eliot Spitzer," CURRENT, 8/8/2012.

111   "Viewpoint with Eliot Spitzer," CURRENT, 6/14/2012.

skilled immigrants.[112] Once the surface is peeled away, it becomes clear that these "jobs bills" are a thinly veiled attempt at pushing through a distinctly right-wing agenda.

With the national debt so high, the country is in great need of a responsible, progressive budget plan that benefits most Americans. Instead, government has offered two competing plans, one mediocre, courtesy of President Obama, and one disastrous, courtesy of Republican Rep. Paul Ryan from Wisconsin. Democracynow.org reports that Obama's $3.7 trillion plan seeks to trim the federal deficit by *cutting or eliminating* some 200 federal programs, many dedicated to *social services and education*, while *increasing military spending* and funding for the construction of nuclear power plants [italics added for emphasis]. Obama's budget would also freeze funding for domestic programs outside of the military for five years. This freeze would cut the deficit by more than $400 billion over the next decade. The plan includes two modest tax hikes for banks and oil companies. It also calls for ending the Bush-era tax cuts for the wealthiest Americans in 2013 and returning the estate tax to its higher 2009 levels.[113] In support of such a measure, an April 2012 CBS News/NYT poll revealed that 56% of Americans would rather see the government spend more and raise taxes as a result, as opposed to 37% who would prefer the government cut spending and lower taxes.[114]

---

[112]   Ibid.

[113]   See http://www.democracynow.org/2011/2/15/obamas_37_trillion_
budget_calls_for?gclid= CIC1xefLmq8CFcVdTAodPjKaZw.

[114]   "The Ed Show," MSNBC, 4/19/2012.

On the other side of the aisle, the Ryan budget plan would drastically exacerbate income inequality in America. It calls for:

- $3.3 trillion in budget cuts to programs for people with low or moderate income;
- $2.4 trillion in cuts to Medicaid and other health care programs;
- $463 billion in cuts to mandatory programs such as Pell grants or social services;
- $291 billion in cuts to discretionary programs;
- $134 billion in cuts to SNAP (formally known as the Food Stamp Program); and
- $2 trillion in cuts to other programs.

These total $5.3 trillion in proposed budget cuts to programs for low-income people.[115] It is worth noting that women make up 70% of all Medicaid beneficiaries, 67% of college students who receive Pell grants, and 67% of adult food stamp recipients, all of whom would be adversely affected by these reductions.[116] If this wasn't bad enough, Ryan's proposed tax cuts give $4.3 trillion of the $5.3 trillion to the wealthy. In particular, his plan provides for:

- A 12.5% cut for wage earners over $1 million (for an average savings of $265,000);
- An 8.8% cut for wage earners between $500,000 and $1 million ($47,000); and
- A 4.8% cut for wage earners between $200,000 and $500,000 ($11,100).

---

[115] See http://www.washingtonpost.com/blogs/ezra-klein/post/paul-ryan-betrays-his-own-views-on-income-inequality/2012/04/03/gIQAJCv2sS_blog.html.

[116] "Hardball with Chris Matthews," MSNBC, 4/13/2012.

Those earning wages between $40,000 and $50,000 would only receive a 1.5% tax cut ($750), and those most in need—wage earners between $10,000 and $20,000—would receive a meager 0.1% cut ($110).[117] This effectively amounts to taking from the poor and middle class and giving to the rich, or in President Obama's words, "social Darwinism."[118] Ahead of a speech at Georgetown University on April 26, Ryan was met by protesters and presented with a letter from 90 faculty members that included the following declaration: "We would be remiss in our duty to you and our students if we did not challenge your continuing misuse of Catholic teaching to defend a budget plan that decimates food programs for struggling families, radically weakens protections for the elderly and sick, and gives more tax breaks to the wealthiest few."[119] According to former Reagan budget director David Stockman, the Ryan plan "isn't a budget. It's the last will and testimony of the Republican party if they continue to advocate these policies."[120] Despite the disadvantages to the president's plan, it is clearly the lesser of two evils.

To further illustrate where Republicans stand with respect to budgetary and legislative policy, at the conservative CPAC conference in February 2012, Grover Norquist, an American lobbyist, influential conservative activist, and

---

[117] See http://www.washingtonpost.com/blogs/ezra-klein/post/paul-ryan-betrays-his-own-views-on-income-inequality/2012/04/03/gIQAJCv2sS_blog.html.

[118] "Hardball with Chris Matthews," MSNBC, 4/3/2012.

[119] "Hardball with Chris Matthews," MSNBC, 4/26/2012.

[120] "Real Time with Bill Maher," HBO, 4/13/2012.

founder and president of Americans for Tax Reform (ATR), laid out in clear and unambiguous terms what his wing of the Republican Party expects from its president:

> We are not auditioning for fearless leader. We don't need a president to tell us what direction to go. We know what direction we want to go. We want the Paul Ryan budget . . . We just need a president to sign this stuff . . . We don't need someone to think it up or design it. We have a House and a Senate. The leadership now for the modern conservative movement for the next 20 years will be coming out of the House and the Senate. Pick a Republican with enough working digits to handle a pen to become President of the United States.[121]

This statement is dumbfounding. Norquist is saying he desires form over substance. Though a mere figurehead is unfit for the position of leader of the free world, it is apparently what Tea Party Republicans want. This is why Mitt Romney is their perfect candidate: he will say and do anything to become president.

During a *Today Show* interview in January 1998, Hillary Clinton complained of a "vast right-wing conspiracy."[122] If the State Policy Network (SPN) is any indication, her views were accurate. As Motherjones.com reveals, "Conceived by the same conservative ideologues who helped found the Heritage Foundation, SPN is a little-known umbrella group with deep ties to the national conservative movement. Its

---

[121] "Hardball with Chris Matthews," MSNBC, 5/2/2012.

[122] "The War Room with Jennifer Granholm," CURRENT, 5/18/2012.

mission is simple: to back a constellation of state-level think tanks loosely modeled after Heritage that promote free-market principles and rail against unions, regulation, and tax increases. By blasting out policy recommendations and shaping lawmakers' positions through briefings and private meetings, these think tanks cultivate cozy relationships with GOP politicians. And there's a long tradition of revolving door relationships between SPN staffers and state governments. While they bill themselves as independent think tanks, SPN's members frequently gather to swap ideas. 'We're all comrades in arms,' the network's board chairman told the *National Review* in 2007.[123]

"Founded in 1992 by businessman and Reagan administration insider Thomas Roe—who also served on the Heritage Foundation's board of trustees for two decades—the group has grown to include 59 'freedom centers,' or affiliated think tanks, in all 50 states . . . According to SPN's website, Roe launched the conservative network 'at the urging' of President Reagan himself as a way to shape state-level policy just as Heritage has influenced federal policy."[124] It is nothing more than a clearinghouse for right-wing think tanks like Heritage, the Heartland Institute, the Mackinac Center, and Americans for Prosperity. All of these organizations promote anti-Democratic policies like voter disenfranchisement and union busting. Furthermore, they receive funding from the infamous Koch brothers. These groups are also behind the ALEC, which plays a role in taking legislation crafted by these think tanks and moving

---

[123] See http://www.motherjones.com/politics/2011/04/state-policy-network-union-bargaining.

[124] Ibid.

it into state houses around the country.[125] Motherjones.com exposes the underlying truth:

> Surveying the political landscape today, Roe's and Reagan's idea couldn't have been more prescient. More than a dozen states are currently considering legislation weakening the clout of organized labor.
>
> In Michigan . . . the Mackinac Center for Public Policy, an SPN member, published a list of four policy recommendations that would give *unelected* "emergency managers" more power to go into municipalities and wipe out union contracts and fire local elected officials, all in the name of repairing broken budgets. All four ended up in Governor Rick Snyder's "financial martial law," as one GOP lawmaker described it. The bill was signed into law in March [2012].
>
> When SPN think tanks are not providing conservative lawmakers with ammo, they're providing them with cover as they take on organized labor. In Wisconsin, as Republican Gov. Scott Walker weathered criticism and sinking approval ratings for his anti-union "repair" bill, the MacIver Institute and Wisconsin Policy Research Institute, both SPN members, rushed to his defense. MacIver lauded Walker's controversial bill as a "step in taming the behemoth" of big government caused by public-sector unions. Meanwhile, a staffer for the Wisconsin Policy Research Institute (and former Wisconsin legislative aide) defended Walker's bill in an error-riddled *New York Times* op-ed as

---

[125] "The War Room with Jennifer Granholm," CURRENT, 5/18/2012.

"fiscally modest, but politically bold." As tens of thousands poured into the streets of Madison to oppose Walker's bill, MacIver even cut a video that dismissed the pro-labor protesters as radicalized communists and socialists.

Tracie Sharp, SPN's president, told *Mother Jones* magazine in an email that member think tanks "set their own policy agendas" and "have always been fiercely independent." But those on the other side of the fight see the think tanks as part of a broader effort. "This is not a grassroots movement to eliminate collective bargaining," says Al Mance, executive director of the Tennessee Education Association, the state's largest teachers union. "This is a national movement, and it's funded by all the conservative moneyed interests."[126]

If ideas such as voter suppression and union busting are so wonderful, if the far right's vision and information are as flawless and true as they purport, why do they hide them behind veiled groups with apple-pie names and hidden super PAC donors? Why not put it out in the open like our founding fathers intended? Could it be because their intentions would wither under the light of truth?[127] Could it be because the public would see them for what they truly are—Tea Party ideologues?

As most Americans know, the United States Postal Service (USPS) is an independent agency of the United

---

[126] See http://www.motherjones.com/politics/2011/04/state-policy-network-union-bargaining.

[127] "The War Room with Jennifer Granholm," CURRENT, 5/18/2012.

States government and one of the few government agencies explicitly authorized by the United States Constitution. It employs over 574,000 workers and operates over 218,000 vehicles. It is the second largest civilian employer in the United States, following Wal-Mart. The USPS is the operator of the largest vehicle fleet in the world. It is legally obligated to serve all Americans, regardless of geography, at uniform prices and quality. With minor exceptions, it has not directly received taxpayer dollars since the early 1980s. The USPS's revenue has dropped sharply over the last decade due to declining mail volume, prompting the agency to look to other sources of revenue while cutting costs to reduce its budget deficit.[128]

Of great significance to this deficit is the Postal Accountability and Enhancement Act of 2006 (PAEA), which obligates the USPS to prefund 75 years worth of future health care benefit payments to retirees within only a 10-year time span—a requirement to which no other government organization is subject. In addition to the weak economy and the diversion of mail to electronic means, the PAEA mandates have had an extraordinary impact on Postal Service finances. As a consequence, it has been charged that the U.S. Postal Service budget crisis of 2011 is, in essence, an artificial one.

To respond to the shortfall, the postmaster general proposed the following:

- The closure of more than 250 mail processing centers;
- The closure of 3,700 post offices,
- The elimination of 100,000 jobs;

---

[128] See http://en.wikipedia.org/wiki/United_States_Postal_Service.

- The termination of Saturday delivery; and
- First class mail delivery delays.

All of this is a direct outcome of the PAEA, passed by the Republican lame-duck session of Congress in 2006 and signed into law by President Bush. As mentioned earlier, the USPS must pay out $5.5 billion in annual advance payments to cover future retiree health benefits as a result. Such payments have added $20 billion in debt to its balance sheet since 2007. Not surprisingly, 2006 was the last year it turned an annual profit. Why is this so? Because Republicans want to kill the Postal Service's unions and subsequently privatize the agency.

The Postal Service is the lifeblood of our country—nearly 175.7 billion pieces of mail were delivered in 2009 alone (excluding ancillary services such as certified mail).[129] Senator Bernie Sanders of Vermont has stated that there are approximately eight million national jobs connected to a strong and effective Postal Service and has also declared that the service is vitally important to American small businesses.[130] Rural America is going to pay a heavy price for the proposed cuts; they will be the first to lose service. Postage rates must rise in part to help fund this unjustified congressional mandate. Dismantling the USPS is at the top of the Republicans' to-do list,[131] and their efforts must be stopped before we lose the service as we know it.

Fortunately, the Senate passed a bill in April 2012 to aid the Postal Service in their time of crisis. In particular,

---

[129] See http://wiki.answers.com/Q/
How_many_pieces_of_mail_are_delivered_each_year_in_the_US.

[130] "The Ed Show," MSNBC, 4/25/2012.

[131] "The Ed Show," MSNBC, 4/17/2012.

the bill offers retirement incentives for 100,000 employees, resulting in a savings of up to $8 billion a year; ensures the continuation of Saturday delivery for the next two years; and makes it harder to close small-town post offices.

Lawmakers, however, do not appear to be in a hurry to proceed. As of this book's publication, the House has still not brought the bill up for a vote, despite a May 15 deadline set by the Postal Service. Failure to meet this deadline resulted in reduced hours at 13,000 post offices nationwide. The threat of closure still looms.[132]

Few Supreme Court decisions have impacted the electoral process more than *Citizens United v. Federal Election Commission* in 2010. In a 5-to-4 ruling, the court "held that the First Amendment prohibited the government from restricting political expenditures by corporations and unions." More specifically, the ruling states that a "provision of the Bipartisan Campaign Reform Act (commonly known as the McCain-Feingold Act) prohibiting unions, corporations and not-for-profit organizations from broadcasting electioneering communications within 60 days of a general election or 30 days of a primary election violates the free speech clause of the First Amendment to the United States Constitution."[133] As Wikipedia explains, "Citizens United has often been credited (or blamed) for the creation of 'super PACs,' political action committees which make no contributions to candidates or parties and so can accept unlimited contributions from individuals, corporations, and unions . . . In addition to indirectly

---

[132] See http://www.savethepostoffice.com/.

[133] See http://en.wikipedia.org/wiki/Citizens_united.

providing support for the creation of super PACs, 'Citizens United' allowed incorporated 501(c)(4) public advocacy groups (such as the National Rifle Association or Sierra Club, or the group Citizens United itself) and trade associations to make expenditures in political races."[134]

Super PACs can accept unlimited contributions from domestic or foreign donors without having to disclose their names. In effect, this blows the campaigning process wide open: corporations and wealthy individuals with very deep pockets can donate any amount they choose to a super PAC. Such contributions dwarf those made by ordinary citizens; for example, one large corporation donating $10 million to a super PAC has the buying power of 400,000 individuals donating $25 each. Democratic Senator Russ Feingold, a lead sponsor of the 2002 Bipartisan Campaign Reform Act, spoke out on the ruling: "This decision was a terrible mistake. Presented with a relatively narrow legal issue, the Supreme Court chose to roll back laws that have limited the role of corporate money in federal elections since Teddy Roosevelt was president."[135] Former Representative Alan Grayson, a Democrat, called it "the worst Supreme Court decision since the Dred Scott case" and said that the court had "opened the door to political bribery and corruption in elections to come."[136],[137]

---

[134] Ibid.

[135] Hunt, Kasie (2010-01-21). "John McCain, Russ Feingold diverge on court ruling." Politico.com.

[136] Baumann, Nick (2010-01-22). "Grayson: Court's Campaign Finance Decision "Worst Since Dred Scott." Mother Jones. Mother Jones and the Foundation for National Progress. Retrieved 2010-01-26.

[137] See http://en.wikipedia.org/wiki/Citizens_united.

A ThinkProgress.org report provides an example of this monetary imbalance: "2012 GOP presidential favorite Mitt Romney has been receiving the support of the Restore Our Future Super PAC. Restore Our Future has been using its millions of dollars to run misleading advertisements about Romney's opponents. NBC has noted that Restore Our Future is 'by far the best-funded of the super PACs backing presidential candidates in the 2012 election' . . . The financial industry loves Romney since Romney is both a former financial executive himself, and wants to repeal the Dodd-Frank financial reform law." [138]

Why is the financial industry putting so much money into Romney's campaign? The answer is simple: return on investment (ROI). It is banking on a Romney election leading to the deregulation of Wall Street. The millionaires and billionaires funding these super PACs are also counting on the following ROIs:

- Tax cuts for the wealthiest Americans;
- Environmental deregulation—new threats to clean air and water;
- Defense contracts—protecting the Pentagon spending budget;
- Corporate welfare—protecting government subsidies for corporations;
- Wall Street deregulation—repeal of the Dodd-Frank law;

---

[138] See http://thinkprogress.org/economy/2012/04/03/457234/ half-romney-super-pac039s-donations-come-from-financial- industry/?mobile=nc.

- Limiting jury award settlements—protecting corporations from being sued for wrongdoing and running over consumers; and
- More oil drilling—even though the country is already drilling now more than ever.[139]

The financial industry knows that if Romney gets elected, he will preserve their financial interests regardless of what benefits the rest of the populace. Citizens United has greatly magnified the battle between the top 1% and the bottom 99%. In effect, control over the election process has shifted away from the voting public to corporations and big-money donors. Millionaires and billionaires can now determine the outcome of elections if they so choose. This brings to mind a campaign poster formerly on the set of *The War Room with Jennifer Granholm*: "Elections that are for sale are not free."

Emissions trading, known more commonly as "cap and trade," is a hotly contested environmental policy. As Wikipedia explains, it is a "market-based approach used to control pollution by providing economic incentives for achieving reductions in the emissions of pollutants. A central authority (usually a governmental body) sets a limit or cap on the amount of a pollutant that may be emitted. The limit or cap is allocated or sold to firms in the form of emissions permits [that] represent the right to emit or discharge a specific volume of the specified pollutant . . . Firms that need to increase their volume of emissions must buy permits from those who require fewer permits . . . The transfer of permits is referred to as a trade. In effect, the

---

[139] "The Ed Show," MSNBC, 5/30/2012.

buyer is paying a charge for polluting, while the seller is being rewarded for having reduced emissions. Thus, in theory, those who can reduce emissions most cheaply will do so, achieving the pollution reduction at the lowest cost to society."[140]

In 2003, John McCain and Sen. Joe Lieberman, then a Democrat, introduced the Climate Stewardship Act, which would have used a similar cap-and-trade approach to reduce carbon pollution linked to global warming. Versions of the bill were reintroduced in 2005 and 2007.[141] In February 2008, McCain observed that "[with] cap-and-trade, there will be incentives for people to reduce greenhouse gas emissions," calling it a "free market approach." Less than two years later, in an April 2009 speech, he made the following declaration: "I will not and cannot align myself with a giant government slush fund . . . It's cap-and-tax, it's cap-and-tax."[142]

During a PolitiFact.com interview on August 18, 2011, Democratic Rep. John Boccieri stated that the cap-and-trade concept was "originally a Republican idea" and expressed frustration with the GOP's current opposition: "Only in Washington can you propose an idea, introduce legislation and then campaign against it. I don't understand what Republicans are doing against this. It was their idea. John McCain introduced cap and trade legislation three times."[143]

---

[140]   See http://en.wikipedia.org/wiki/Cap_and_trade.

[141]   http://www.politifact.com/ohio/statements/2010/sep/13/
john-boccieri/democratic-rep-john-boccieri-invokes-gop-sen-john-/.

[142]   "The Rachel Maddow Show," MSNBC, 4/5/2012.

[143]   See http://www.politifact.com/ohio/statements/2010/sep/13/
john-boccieri/democratic-rep-john-boccieri-invokes-gop-sen-john-/.

How can Republicans fully support an environmental policy only to turn around and reject it? Because they are beholden to big oil corporations and energy producers. The party's shift to the far right during the 2010 midterm elections corresponded with legislative attacks on the environment. In only the first year after taking control of the House of Representatives, Republicans voted to strip environmental protections more than 150 times.[144] Two examples of anti-environmental legislation introduced by the highly conservative House are the EPA Regulatory Relief Act and the Cement Sector Regulatory Relief Act. Democratic Rep. John Lewis has identified the detrimental effects of these acts: "They both nullify EPA requirements for industrial boilers, incinerators, and cement plants to reduce their emissions of toxic air pollutants, including well-known extremely harmful chemicals like mercury. They both weaken EPA's ability to issue standards that could revive a mandate for cleaner air, allow polluting plants to indefinitely delay reductions in toxic air pollution, and set no deadline for compliance. Altogether 9,100 lives are lost for every year these pollution reductions are delayed."[145]

As for the advantages of emissions trading, Brookings. edu made the following report: "The real payoff from a domestic cap-and-trade system is that it could pave the way for global action toward emission reductions along the lines that were discussed at the Copenhagen climate change summit in December [2009]. If there are global emissions reductions like those spelled out in the Copenhagen Accord, then the domestic benefits would easily exceed the domestic

---

[144]   "The Rachel Maddow Show," MSNBC, 4/5/2012.

[145]   See http://johnlewis.house.gov/press-release/rep-john-lewis-votes-against-damaging-environmental-legislation.

costs. The critics of cap-and-trade have been correct all along. It would impose costs on the U.S. economy. What they have failed to notice, however, is that the projected benefits are larger than these costs."[146] While cap and trade would probably result in a net increase in electricity bills, it would represent the first large-scale reduction in carbon dioxide levels. Planting trees alone is not going to solve the problem. Global warming will continue to persist and grow until America addresses CO_2 emissions on a national scale.

I will close out this topic with commentary on carbon emissions from former Governor Eliot Spitzer:

> So let me get this straight: [on August 8, 2012] we found out that July was the hottest month on record. Richard Muller, a University of California physics professor, McArthur fellow, and former climate change skeptic whose research was funded by the Koch brothers, concluded recently " . . . global warming was real and that the prior estimates of the rate of warming were correct. I'm now going a step further: humans are almost entirely the cause." And Dr. James Hansen, the Director of NASA's Goddard Institute for Space Studies and father of climate change science, wrote this past week a peer reviewed research he had just completed that his analysis shows that " . . . for the extreme hot weather of the recent past, there is virtually no explanation other than climate change." The pace and scale of the impact of global

---

[146] See http://www.brookings.edu/opinions/2010/0730_climate_change_greenstone.aspx.

warming are accelerating and devastating. The time for action is limited as we approach a tipping point beyond which the opportunity to reverse the damage of CO_2 emissions will disappear. And what are we talking about in our presidential campaigns? Obamaloney and Romneyhood. Silliness has taken over; the capacity to raise tough issues dissipated if not gone entirely. Climate change appears to have fallen off the political agenda entirely. Yet there is an answer for either candidate courageous enough to take the first step; an answer steep in conservative economics: the theory that companies that pollute should be taxed so that a product's cost to society is reflected in the price of that product. Milton Friedman and Richard Posner agree on this point. The idea proposed by Hansen is simple: a fee on carbon emissions collected from fossil fuel companies with 100% of the money rebated to legal residents on a per capita basis. It is simple, would move us away from carbon-based fuels, would cost most consumers nothing, and would stimulate innovation in the clean energy sector. Right now, in contrast, we are subsidizing fossil fuels to the tune of hundreds of billions of dollars a year while the greatest minds in science agree that we are destroying our planet. It is not a matter of ideology to say that this makes no sense. It is a matter of simple conservative economics.[147]

---

[147] "Viewpoint with Eliot Spitzer," CURRENT, 8/9/2012.

Chapter 6
Conclusion

As is the case with the general electorate, there are moderate and extreme factions in both the Democratic and Republican parties. At different points in time, each has risen to power within their respective party. As of 2012, it is safe to say moderates are largely in control of the Democratic Party. Despite what Republicans claim, Democrats are not as liberal as they were in the 1960s. The Republican Party, meanwhile, is clearly controlled by extremists. The Tea Party has pushed Republicans farther to the right than at any other point in their history. Social conservatives are trying to return the country to the mores and standards of the 1950s. Gone are moderates like Gerald Ford and Nelson Rockefeller. Moderates differ from Tea Party conservatives in that they are temperate in their approach to issues. Compromises were once feasible between moderate Republicans and Democrats. Unfortunately, party members are as polarized today as they have ever been.

To underscore this point, Congress recently saw its most unproductive year in modern history. In 2011 it passed only 80 bills, fewer than in any other session since year-end recording began in 1947. Furthermore, an analysis by the *Washington Times* of such factors as time spent in debate, number of conference reports produced, and votes taken on the House and Senate floors found that the 112th Congress set a record for legislative futility by accomplishing less in 2011 than any other year in history.[148] This paralysis cannot continue; clearly a change is required, and the best opportunity will come at the ballot box this November.

There is no better example of the existing impasse than deficit reduction. Strategies for reducing the deficit typically include spending cuts and raising taxes. The latter measure is virtually impossible in today's political climate. As of late 2011, anti-tax activist Grover Norquist co-opted 238 of 242 House Republicans and 41 of 47 Senate Republicans to sign ATR's "Taxpayer Protection Pledge." By agreeing to this pledge, members promised to "oppose any and all efforts to increase the marginal income tax rate for individuals and/ or businesses."[149] Since Norquist's pledge binds signatories to oppose deficit reduction agreements that include any element of tax increases, some Republican deficit hawks now retired from office have stated that Norquist has actually become an obstacle to deficit reduction.[150]

The Budget Control Act of 2011, established to prevent the default that could have resulted from the 2011 debt-ceiling crisis, resulted in the creation of the U.S Congressional Joint Select Committee on Deficit Reduction. The committee was charged with issuing a recommendation by November 23, 2011 for at least $1.5 trillion in additional deficit reduction steps to be undertaken over a 10-year period. Possible areas for examination by the committee comprised revenue increases, including raising taxes; tax

---

[148] See http://www.washingtontimes.com/news/2012/jan/15/congress-logs-most-futile-legislative-year-on-reco/?page=all.

[149] "Taxpayer Protection Pledge" (PDF). Americans for Tax Reform. 2011. Retrieved December 11, 2011.

[150] See http://en.wikipedia.org/wiki/Grover_Norquist.

reforms, such as simplifying the tax code and eliminating some tax breaks and loopholes; military spending cuts; and measures to reform and slow the growth of entitlement programs, including Medicare, Medicaid, and Social Security. On November 21, the committee concluded its work, issuing a statement that began with the following: "After months of hard work and intense deliberations, we have come to the conclusion today that it will not be possible to make any bipartisan agreement available to the public before the committee's deadline."[151],[152] In the end, Republicans refused to raise taxes and Democrats refused to trim entitlement programs. Ultimately, no compromises were made, and the more radical factions in each party won out.

This sentiment is enforced by congressional scholars Thomas E. Mann and Norman J. Ornstein, who wrote the following in a *Washington Post* op-ed:

> The GOP has become an insurgent outlier in American politics. It is ideologically extreme; scornful of compromise; unmoved by conventional understanding of facts, evidence and science; and dismissive of the legitimacy of its political opposition. While the Democrats may have moved from their 40-yard line to their 25, the Republicans

---

[151] "Statement from Co-Chairs of the Joint Select Committee on Deficit Reduction." deficitreduction.gov. November 21, 2011. Retrieved January 30, 2012.

[152] See http://en.wikipedia.org/wiki/United_States_Congress_Joint_Select_Committee_on_Deficit_Reduction.

have gone from their 40 to somewhere behind their goalpost.[153]

As far as extremes go, both parties have their shortcomings. On the Democratic side, bleeding heart liberals represent incessant Pollyannas no matter the circumstance, even when confronted with problems that have difficult solutions. On the Republican side, staunch conservatives remain entrenched in the past despite evidence to the contrary of their beliefs. Both are difficult to negotiate with and unyielding in their views.

A better understanding of the two factions involved can be gained through definition. Te jen of SciForums.com aptly defines *liberal* as "not limited to or by established, traditional, orthodox, or authoritarian attitudes, views, or dogmas. Favoring proposals for reform, open to new ideas for progress, and tolerant of the ideas and behavior of others; broad-minded";[154] and free from prejudice or bigotry.[155] *Bleeding heart* is defined as "a person who makes an ostentatious or excessive display of pity or concern for others."[156] An example of bleeding heart liberalism is traditional welfare, a failed system.

Dictionary.com defines *conservative* as "disposed to preserve existing [views,] conditions, institutions, etc., or to restore traditional ones, and to limit change."[157] *Staunch* is defined as "firm or steadfast in principle, adherence,

---

153   "Hardball with Chris Matthews," MSNBC, 5/3/2012.

154   See http://www.sciforums.com/Define-Bleeding-Heart-Liberal-t-36764.html.

155   See http://dictionary.reference.com/browse/liberal?s=t.

156   See http://dictionary.reference.com/browse/bleeding+heart?s=t.

157   See http://dictionary.reference.com/browse/conservative?s=t.

[allegiance], etc."[158] An example of staunch conservativism is the National Prohibition Act, which led to the 18th Amendment, and trickle-down economics, also failed policies.

If left to their own devices, Democrats invariably raise taxes in part to help pay for costly social programs. This tendency, however, has been mitigated by the rise of an exceptionally conservative Congress in 2010. Even in that midterm election year, there was pressure on the president to extend the Bush-era tax cuts another two years through 2012. The 112th Congress' steadfast insistence on rejecting any form of tax increase has limited what the Obama administration can do in this regard. The focus has alternately shifted to addressing income inequality by keeping the Bush tax cuts for the poor and middle class and raising taxes on those earning more than $250,000 a year instead. Such an increase will have to wait until after the 2012 elections because the current Congress will not allow it.

A classic example of overreach on both sides of the aisle is health care legislation. On the liberal side, there is the Clinton Health Care Plan of 1993 (a.k.a. Hillarycare), a poorly conceived universal health care proposal that was soundly defeated by Congress in 1994. In 2005, referring to her previous efforts at health care reform, Hillary Clinton remarked: "I learned some valuable lessons about the legislative process, the importance of bipartisan cooperation and the wisdom of taking small steps to get a

---

[158]   See http://dictionary.reference.com/browse/staunch?s=t.

big job done."[159] In 2007, she reflected on her role in 1993 and 1994: "I think that both the process and the plan were flawed. We were trying to do something that was very hard to do, and we made a lot of mistakes."[160],[161]

The conservatives oppose the Affordable Care Act of 2010 (a.k.a. Obamacare), the best health care reform plan to be proposed in a century. It contains many long-sought-after benefits such as preventing insurers from dropping coverage when people get sick, ending discrimination based on preexisting conditions, ending lifetime caps on benefits, charging women the same rate for the same coverage as men, etc. (the various provisions are detailed in Chapter 3). Republicans did everything in their power to defeat the bill in Congress, kicking and screaming every step of the way until its historic passage. They even opposed the individual mandate, a concept they formerly championed as far back as 1989 and as late as 2009,[162] and brought a case against the mandate all the way to the Supreme Court, two years after the law's inception.

The court subsequently upheld the mandate and all but one of the law's key provisions on June 28, 2012, thus rendering it constitutional. The decision was 5 to 4, with Chief Justice John Roberts casting the deciding vote in the face of intense opposition from his conservative

---

[159]   "The Evolution of Hillary Clinton," New York Times, July 13, 2005. Accessed June 8, 2007.

[160]   Toner, Robin and Kornblut, Anne. "Wounds Salved, Clinton Returns to Health Care," The New York Times, June 10, 2006. Accessed June 8, 2007.

[161]   See http://en.wikipedia.org/wiki/Clinton_health_care_plan_of_1993.

[162]   "The Rachel Maddow Show," MSNBC, 6/22/2012.

counterparts. In so doing, he brought honor to his position on the bench.

While the court ruled that the federal government does not have the power to order people to buy health insurance, it does have the power to impose a tax on those without health insurance. The 250 million Americans who already have health insurance will be able to keep it; the law will only make it more secure and affordable. As for the 30 million Americans who do not yet have health insurance, starting in 2014, this law will offer an array of quality affordable private health insurance plans to choose from. Those who cannot afford the premiums will receive a credit to help pay for them. Furthermore, small businesses previously unable to do so can now offer affordable health care to their employees. Despite what Republicans say, the law creates four million jobs, reduces the deficit, lowers costs to individuals, improves quality, and expands coverage. Every Democratic president since Franklin Roosevelt has tried to implement health care reform unsuccessfully. Most of the other industrialized democracies in the world have it. The dream of fair and affordable health care has finally been realized in this country.[163]

Indeed, there are advantages and disadvantages to both parties. Your selection on the ballot should take into account the various issues impacting America. When I vote, I take into consideration the fact that Republicans seek to disenfranchise minority, young, elderly, and poor voters; perpetuate and exacerbate income inequality; exhibit a comprehensive disregard for the environment and the EPA; advocate unfair health care practices benefitting insurance

---

[163] "The Ed Show," MSNBC, 6/28/2012.

companies; decimate social programs; roll back 50 years of women's health and equal pay advances; destroy Medicare as we know it; dismantle labor unions; recklessly deregulate financial industries; fight wars based on ideological grounds; and promote lax gun laws that take us back to the days of the Wild West.

In the end, you must vote your conscience. This book presents relevant topics to help guide you through the democratic process. Deciding which party and candidate will usher in the kind of change you are looking for requires an ability to see through often-slanderous campaign ads and identify a candidate's *real* intentions. Your choice should be based on unbiased news and the underlying issues in a campaign. Democracy works best when the electorate is informed. Read the newspaper, watch the evening news, and study analysis from experts in the field. Empower yourself. Only then will your vote carry its full meaning.